THE

THINGS

MAGGIE BOXEY

3

THE

THINGS

RISE
BOOKS

A PRACTICAL PATH TO COLLECTIVE RECOVERY

**RISE
BOOKS**

Copyright © 2024 by Maggie Boxey

Jacket design by Thunderwing Studio
Interior design by Pauline Neuwirth, Neuwirth & Associates, Inc.

Library of Congress Cataloging-in-Publication Data Available Upon Request

ISBN 978-1-959524-02-1 (hardcover)
ISBN 978-1-959524-09-0 (eBook)

Printed in the United States of America
First Edition
10 9 8 7 6 5 4 3 2 1

To my Daddy+,

Thank you for The 3 Things and for encouraging me to share them with the world.

Love,
Your 3½-pound baby girl

CONTENTS

PART THREE:
Glorify God in All That You Do

Introduction

I sat perched on a white folding chair under the tent, waiting for the speech to begin. It was my brother's high school graduation at St. Andrew's Sewanee in Tennessee. A draft from the mountain breeze bit through my sweater, which was more for show than function, as I straightened then slouched my spine in my best attempt to look cool and unbothered. My floral-print maxi skirt blew against my knock-off Doc Martens, highlighting the contrast between my fifteen-year-old vulnerability and the sour look on my face, a perfect representation of my flowers and combat spirit. I was still sulking because Mama made me leave my Walkman behind, along with my well-worn Indigo Girls cassette tape. This was the mid-1990s after all, when the Indigo Girls were the emotional support soundtrack for every angry, lonely, out-of-place girl just trying to survive the end of the century in America. The yellow-and-white-striped tent created a stuffy greenhouse effect and cast a sunny vibe on the event, making me feel hot and cold at the same time.

My grandfather was supposed to be the speaker that day. He'd been headmaster of the school for over twenty years. Three weeks before his speech, he unexpectedly passed away. Only one person could fill his shoes that sunny Friday morning, the man I've called "Daddy" since I could say my first words. My father was also an Episcopal priest, so he was the obvious replacement.

As a priest's kid, Daddy's sermons and speeches made me feel an excited sort of dread. Stories of our family often washed over the congregation when he spoke. Seeing as how my grandfather had been headmaster, my mom and dad met at this school, my brother was graduating, and soon after the graduation, we'd be burying my grandfather's ashes within throwing distance from where I sat, there was no getting around how deeply our family was woven into the community. I knew the Martin family would be mentioned.

Daddy walked out onto the stage, and though I have long forgotten the details of his speech, its main points have become the guiding lights of my life—and my reason for writing this book. Right there in that tent, Daddy's words pierced through the muggy air, through my floral combat armor, past the Indigo Girls song playing on repeat in my head, and into my soul. He shared that all of life, all of love, all of our loss and joy and participation in this fleeting, beautiful existence, could be distilled down to 3 Things:

YOU ARE PART OF A FAMILY.

BE TRUE TO YOURSELF.

GLORIFY GOD IN ALL THAT YOU DO.

Tears of pride stung my eyes as I watched how beautifully Daddy had delivered this message in the midst of his own raw grief. I felt the gravity of his words. After we left the warm glow of the tent and came home, The 3 Things took on a life of their own. They became our family prayer, our motto, the greeting we would offer each other upon arrival and departure, the mission statement of our family, not just as leaders in the church, but within our own household. The 3 Things were the guiding force of how my family expected us to live our lives.

Even when I didn't want them to be.

Because in the years after that speech, The 3 Things stopped being the enlightening touchstone of the best way to live our lives and instead, became the frustrating and, eventually, heart-breaking reminder of how I was failing to live mine.

"Bye, Mama and Daddy! Love you!" I would shout from the front door after whizzing past my parents in the living room. I paused briefly to make sure I had everything I needed for the night: pager (yes, a pager), check; cigarettes, check; nineties crop top, check; keys to my 1981 Volkswagen Rabbit convertible, check.

I'd be so close to the freedom on the other side of the door, when Daddy would call out:

"Maggie! What are the 3 Things?"

I didn't have time for preaching. I would blurt out the 3 Things as fast as possible with a huff and exaggerated eye roll:

"I am part of a family, will be true to myself, and glorify God in all that I do. Now can I go?"

Satisfied that he had done his duty in both embarrassing me and in setting a sacred intention over my evening, Daddy would send me on my way. They thought I was heading out to a wholesome slumber party with parental supervision, when really, I was going to binge drink in the dark shadows of town with unknown friends and consequences. This became a pattern, more worn out than that Indigo Girls cassette tape in my Walkman. I'd rattle off the 3 Things and walk away from the safety of home with a sinking stone of guilt in the pit of my stomach. Then I'd venture out to the shameful corners of my secret world to live the opposite of those truths. It would be twenty-five hard, traumatic years before I truly came to understand, embrace, and live by the 3 Things.

Over the years, I began to realize that the 3 Things aren't just for me (or my biological family), they are universal truths for everyone. We all have access to them. And whether we know them already or not, we are already living them.

As I began to heal from my years of drowning in addiction and depression, I noticed that when I was aligned with the 3 Things in my life, I flourished. But when I lived my life in opposition to them, I withered. I stopped trusting that there's a divine order or energy. My connection to family frayed. And I began to question my value and worth in this world. If we don't feel valuable and worthy, we will ultimately sabotage ourselves. For years, I lived the 3 Things in reverse. Instead of being part of a family, I isolated myself from the world. Rather than glorifying God, I felt unworthy of God's love. I relied on foxhole prayers and Hail Mary church visits to try and save myself from the suffocating shadow of guilt and remorse that followed me everywhere. Rather than being true to myself, I lived true to people-pleasing and did whatever would make me desirable or attractive to others. While I did good deeds, my motives were self-protective; they certainly weren't selfless. And it all finally led to an alcoholic, suicidal bottom.

None of it was sustainable.

After I got sober and started living the 3 Things (made possible by working through a twelve-step program), I wanted everyone to have a program. I love that I get to share this path and this idea that we all have the chance to heal with my community.

> The way we get everyone free is one at a time, embarking on a road to recovery, whatever that looks like for each of us.

Being a white woman from the South, living in rural southern Georgia, I am very clear that the 3 Things were not merely about personal development and living my best life, but about creating more justice in the world. The model of *community*, self-awareness through *contemplation*, and *celebration* can be applied to the collective, but only if we as individuals do the work. This is the practical path to collective recovery.

What I discovered is that the 3 Things are far more fluid than I initially gave them credit for. I shrugged them off as Christian words coming from a Christian preacher (my Daddy), which they are, but they are also a practical path to my own recovery, to all of our recoveries. And I don't just mean from drugs and alcohol. Because the 3 Things give us the space to honor family, however we define it, to be true to ourselves, no matter what people might think of us, and glorify God in all that we do, no matter how we define God.

When I started jotting down ideas for *The 3 Things,* I was pregnant with my second child. For years, I nagged Daddy to write the book because it couldn't be me who was supposed to do it, could it? That child is now eleven as I write this. Time got away from me, as it does, but The 3 Things did not. It stayed with me, filling a beautiful decade full of the profound experiences I've had because I applied this stuff to my own messy, incredible life.

I got sick in July 2020 with a virus that was most likely COVID-19 (the testing available in my area wasn't always reliable at that time). To complicate the diagnosis, the virus attacked my nervous system (and not my respiratory system, as many had experienced). My skin buzzed and my head hurt worse than any hangover times ten. I suffered air hunger (gasping for breath with no apparent cause) after walking to the kitchen or bathroom from the bed where I spent my days wondering if this was it for me. I went from running half-marathons to being bedridden in a matter of days.

Sometime that September, I dropped to my knees in desperation. I prayed to the divine to please save me, heal me, or kill me because I couldn't go on like that anymore. My answer came in the form of The 3 Things. At that moment, I knew I was the one meant to write this book. The outline flowed from my pen as I sat in stillness, in contemplation.

Through my examination and writing of *The 3 Things*, I implemented recovery practices to help me heal my debilitating illness. I reintroduced play and creativity through watercolors, at first with my children, and then on my own. I connected with a long-lost younger part of myself that wanted to be a writer and artist when I grew up. I began asking myself as I moved through my days, "Am I honoring the gift of being part of a family? Am I being true to myself? Am I glorifying God in all that I do?" My prayer to be healed came in an unexpected way. I healed from the inner wells of spirit outward. However, there was more happening in my body than I realized.

Six months later, at the age of forty-two, I was diagnosed with a benign brain tumor. Another six months after that, I had a craniotomy to remove the golf-ball-sized tumor from the groove at the very front of my brain. Before surgery, Mama asked me, "Aren't you afraid to be alone?" COVID-19 precautions limited loved ones from joining in the pre-op area and she was concerned about me braving it by myself.

"I'm not alone," I said without thinking. "I'm not alone because I have the 3 Things. I am part of a family, I will be true to myself, and I will glorify God in all that I do."

As it happened, the hospital loosened the COVID-19 precautions to allow one family member into pre-op, and I was able to hold my husband's hand through all the waiting. As they wheeled me into surgery, the nurses asked if I'd like to listen to music. I told them to play the Indigo Girls.

For me, the 3 Things aren't just about family, me, and God, they're about rediscovering community, contemplation, and celebration. And when I widened my understanding of the 3 Things, I understood that those three deeper principles in action allowed me to live in collective recovery. Because we can't do it alone.

This book is for those who have been on the road of recovery for a bit, those who are lost and wanting, and those who don't yet know they are worthy and enough. It's for the floral and combat-booted fifteen-year-old girl sitting under that graduation tent two-and-a-half decades ago, who felt she could never get it right. The trail of seeking and living by the whole-hearted principles of the 3 Things is a long, crooked journey—one that might just bring us all closer to God, closer to ourselves, closer to community, and of course, closer to fine.

PART ONE

You Are Part of a Family

Have the imagination to see our community fully restored. When we engage with those around us, we will see humanity in everyone. It's not them versus us. Our community is all of us. But the end is reconciliation; the end is redemption; the end is the creation of the beloved community. It is this type of spirit and this type of love that can transform opposers into friends. It is this type of understanding goodwill that will transform the deep gloom of the old age into the exuberant gladness of the new age. It is this love that will bring about miracles in the hearts of men.

—Martin Luther King Jr.,
"Facing the Challenge of a New Age," 1956

CHAPTER ONE

What Is Family?

In rural America, before the Industrial Revolution, the barn was an integral part of the family system. The barn ensured survival through harsh winters and in times of famine. It's where the animals took shelter, where hay and food and tools were stored. When a family needed a barn but didn't have the resources to build one, the community would come together for a barn raising. They'd all chip in their time and supplies to get the barn built, their labor unpaid, knowing that when their time of need arrived, all present would return the gesture. Those same families would share bounty from harvests, they would barter and trade goods among them, depending on their individual needs and gifts. Kinfolk would live in the same place, generation after generation, and the community grew along with the families. The old definitions of family always included the community.

Being a part of a family circle means you are a part of something bigger than yourself. It means responsibility and accountability to your neighbors and wider community. It's who you call when the shit hits the fan and who you answer when their shit hits the fan. Within family, there is generosity of spirit and resources. There is unity. Unconditional love. Warmth. Nurturing. Support. Hope. Safety. It's who we cry out to, who we reach for when we're hurting. Family surrounds us, protecting us when we're vulnerable, at risk, or under attack; and who we surround and protect in return. It's those we show our report card to, who cheer for us, and who we uplift and reassure, both in times of celebration and tragedy.

For most of my life, family was defined as blood, those related to me by DNA. For me, family was comprised of the ones you come home to after a hard day, the ones with strong shoulders to lean on and have a good cry. It also included the ones I disappointed and was scared of when I didn't come home at my 10:00 p.m. curfew because I stayed out all night drinking and trespassing at the zoo or the nearby park. Family is who paid the bills and provided. I would later find that it's also who keeps you tethered when you're drifting away from the world.

Over the years, my definition of family evolved. When I went to summer camp at Honey Creek, I met a group of girls who looked like me, acted like me, and felt all the feelings, just like me. We would sit around the common room with our favorite camp counselor making friendship bracelets and belting out the Indigo Girls—"Closer to Fine," "Kid Fears," and "Land of Canaan." It was within the walls of that common room that my idea of family grew to include these core memory makers. When I joined the Navy, my idea of family grew again, including the people marching beside me to carry out our mission in training, and in the fleet. They were the people who were still hanging around when I was at my lowest, medically retired from the Navy. My view of family expanded again when I was newly divorced, losing custody of my child to my husband because of my actions and instability, and entering recovery. Family, as it turns out, extends beyond the nuclear bonds we know in our youth, and becomes a diverse, growing, shifting web of souls who embrace you at your highest and support you at your lowest.

> It becomes a collection of circles, some overlapping, and some connecting you to the next circle of community.

Sometimes it's easier to define something by what it is not. When I'm not a part of a family, I'm alone. I'm isolated. I'm different. I don't belong. I'm vulnerable to attack. Who am I when I don't see others as family? I'm afraid. I'm suspicious. I'm on high alert, ever vigilant and exhausted, with no rest. I'm anxious, angry, opinionated, rigid, and judgmental. Without family, I subscribe to the lie that I'm fine on my own and I don't need anyone. It's me against an uncaring and unjust world.

But when we see our whole community as family, there is no us versus them. We are interconnected. There is no hoarding of resources. There is plenty because the community shares in times of need. When we offer love and support, we are more able to receive love and support. When we allow *all* to be part of our family, our community, we fully grasp the reconciliation and healing that comes with unconditional love and generosity of spirit. We experience the modern-day barn raisings of transformation and collective recovery.

OUR FAMILIES OF ORIGIN

It got hot quick in south Georgia and there wasn't a whisper of air-conditioning for miles. Mama would spritz herself with a spray bottle in front of a fan to stay cool. Even in the heat, she was happy, she was working, pregnant with her second baby, and surrounded by family. She'd called her belly Maggie Lee all through her first pregnancy, though Maggie Lee turned out to be my big brother John. This time, she was certain she'd have a Maggie. She worked as a teacher in a small south Georgia town called Ocilla. After finishing her teaching degree at Mercer, she and Daddy moved back home to live close to family in Fitzgerald, Georgia—right next to family, to be exact. Grandmama and Papa lived in the house across the alley from our apartment, in what we have always called the Big House.

The apartment wasn't all that nice or fancy, but it was home, what would soon be my first home. My mama's brother, Uncle Philip, and his wife, Marion, lived in the apartment below us, until they bought and remodeled their own home, one house and one street over from the Big House. The church was just a block away and the grocery store was one more block down from that. Wild chickens roamed around town, still do. It was an everyday thing to see little flocks of chicken families crossing the road. Our entire family would meet at least once a week at the Big House for supper—cubed steak with grits, gravy, and peas; Manwich; or pot roast and potatoes.

Mama started having contractions on a Friday during summer break. She was told not to worry, to get some rest and drink water. That Saturday, Daddy went river rafting in Dublin, Georgia, about an hour and a half drive from where we lived in Fitzgerald. His four-man team won their race and Daddy got "fall-off-the-barstool drunk" at the postrace celebration. He stumbled in at 2:00 a.m. to find Mama was still having contractions.

At 6:00 a.m., the contractions were stronger, more serious, more regular.

"Hallock! You've got to get up!" she yelled, trying to remain calm, but this was not the time for his ass to be drunk. "Get up! It's serious!"

"Let me sleep it off, baby. You're not due for another six weeks!" Daddy mumbled. He had a point; I wasn't due until August 18, and it was before dawn on June 25.

Words weren't getting through to him, so she brought in the reinforcement of a plastic Wiffle Ball bat. "Get up! Get up! Get up!" Each exclamation landing a blow. "Dammit Hallock! This baby is coming and if you don't get up now, I'm leaving without you!"

Ironically, Mama's doctor was at a conference to learn about birthing premature babies in Atlanta. Dr. Hammond was the resident on duty when they arrived at the hospital around 9:00 a.m. Mama was scheduled for a sonogram the following Monday because she was so big, but that wouldn't be necessary. It was time. At 10:46 a.m., out I came, all 3.5 pounds of me.

Daddy ran out to tell everyone, "It's a girl!"

But then he was called back into the delivery room.

"There's another one in here!" Dr. Hammond yelled. They got the surprise of a lifetime when my twin brother Jacob was born. Daddy ran back out to the waiting room and yelled, "It's a boy! We have a girl *and* a boy!" The room ignited in pure shock and joy. Grandmama couldn't stop laughing, she was so tickled.

My brother John was two when we were born. My parents called from the hospital to give him the surprise news. His reply was, "THERE'S TWO'D OF UM?!"

Because of my tiny size, they rushed me away as soon as my toes and fingers were counted. My twin, Jacob, was four pounds and looked healthier than me. So, Mama and Daddy got to do a little bit of bonding with Jacob while I was doing my first bout of recovery.

It would be thirty-six hours before he died.

They tried to save Jacob, transferring him to a larger hospital in Macon, Georgia. Daddy raced over there, leaving me and Mama in the hospital at Fitzgerald. His dear family friend, Ed Bacon, who was a Baptist preacher and dean of students at Mercer University at the time, met him at the hospital. But when Daddy arrived, Jacob was already gone. Ed was there with Daddy, and they prayed over Jacob. My grandfather, an Episcopal priest, arrived the next day and baptized me in the hospital, as they weren't sure if I'd live either.

I don't know how it could possibly feel to come home from the hospital with one baby after giving birth to two. Mama was too sick to follow us around, complications from birth and grief, I imagine. I was the baby she had to learn how to love during the worst imaginable time of her life. It was Mama and me, there in the beginning, learning how to survive together. I slept in a clothes drawer next to her bed, and she laid awake making sure I was breathing. Mama always said that I had an extra amount of grace, a superpower that I got from my twin Jacob. In his short life, he taught us all about love and community, and how to live through loss.

On the day of Jacob's funeral, Daddy turned back to see cars wrapped around the block showing up for our family in our struggle, our time of need. It was a barn raising of grief, each of our community members shouldering a two-by-four of pain and raising our resilience. Daddy considers that the moment he realized he was not alone and part of a community—a family. He would go on to get sober, accept a calling to the priesthood, and eventually give the 3 Things speech at my brother's graduation in 1994.

As I grew, Mama would ask me if I missed him, but I didn't know how to answer. I grew up with the nagging feeling something was missing, that I was different and followed by a shadow I couldn't name.

I wanted to feel Jacob, to say, "Yes, Mama, I miss him," or "Yes, Mama, he's with me." The truth is, I was so uncomfortable in my skin that I couldn't even bear to talk about him. I lived behind a painful veil through which my parents saw my entrance into their world. This was my irrefutable evidence that something was wrong with me. My parents couldn't celebrate me and my existence without feeling the weight of their sadness. Because the day they gained a daughter was also the day they lost a son.

And that is my family of origin.

In comic books, origin stories are the point at which the superhero realizes their powers after a tragedy or a near-death experience, such as the bite from a radioactive spider or the wrongful death of a loved one. Some superheroes can fly or cling to walls. My power was more subtle than that. I got the power of grace. The comic book origin story sparks a turning point, a pivotal moment we can tie to the character's life as the moment where everything changed. I should have known I was in for the long haul when my first pivotal moment happened so early.

Families of origin work the same way. In these moments of tragedy and pain, they offer us the opportunity to grow or be overwhelmed by the origin stories they offer us.

> For troubled superheroes like us, these pivotal moments either bring us closer to our purpose or further into the dark, which can also bring us closer to our purpose.

Our families can be circles of strength and comfort. Or they can be sources of pain. Often, they are both. Either way, they provide us profound lessons about humanity—theirs and our own.

JUST 'CAUSE IT'S A CIRCLE DOESN'T MEAN IT CAN'T BREAK

For some of us, the word "family" is synonymous with pride, tradition, and obligation. For others, it's about love, nurturing, and a place to go for the holidays. However, for many, the word "family" brings up pain and trauma, and holidays or not, we'd rather not go there. And to really complicate matters, for some of us, it is all of these definitions at the same time.

We evolve and adapt to stay safe in our families of origin and first communities. The mechanisms we develop to survive and belong work for us—until they don't. People-pleasing and being a chameleon was paramount for me. Making sure I fit in, even at my own expense, was essential for my survival.

The truth is, our planetary human family is dysfunctional. We avoid communication in order to keep the peace. The paths of society are loaded with eggshells, and we're all walking on them. We walk around, bumping into each other, passing around our trauma and our lies and our burdens and our debt and our dysfunction. Our denial of the past. Our racism. Our intolerance. Our rugged individualism. Our lack of trust. Toxic masculinity. Victim mentality. PTSD. Mental illness. White supremacy. Alcoholism. Workaholism. All of the "isms," the ones that are glaring and the ones that we can dress up as functioning and desirable traits on résumés (perfectionism, anybody?). We pick up the belief systems of our parents and the generational curses of our ancestors. And we throw it all in a blender and call it a family. Then we take all of those isms, curses, and dysfunction out to our communities.

But with the thorns of dysfunction, there are also some fruits that grow from our family systems. I know that my parents did a lot of work and therapy over the years, and my kids will benefit from the growth and work I'm doing now. Generational curses get passed down. But so does healing.

The Bible says, "If one part suffers, every part suffers. If one part is honored, every part rejoices with it" (Corinthians 12:26).

When you suffer—while I may not share your lived experience—if I'm truly part of a family, I am affected by your suffering. I invite us all to see humanity as one body, one family, one community. And what is this planet, but one big, beautiful circle (technically it's a sphere, but you get the point). It is possible to rebuild our broken circles, to have the imagination to see our community fully restored. People love quoting Dr. Martin Luther King Jr. There are go-to quotes that have been conveniently plucked out to fit a shallow narrative. But in truth, his deeper message was inconvenient for a lot of people. Because he preached about experiencing the suffering of others as our own. He wasn't about passive love. His message was about action, about fighting for all the members of our human family to have the freedom to live their lives with dignity.

When we treat each other as family, only then will we be fulfilling the promise of Dr. King, where there will be exuberant gladness and miracles in the hearts of men! But it's not that easy. Dr. King's message of love has been oversimplified.

In modern times, family is complicated, and it can be a struggle to love in situations of dysfunction, oppression, addiction, and chaos.

MODERN FAMILY

Our family of origin provides us with what we need to grow. Some of the soil is nourishing, and some is toxic. If you grew up in an alcoholic home like I did, you likely developed superpowers quite early, like I had to do. When I use the term "alcoholic home," I mean there was no particular abuse or neglect, or anything willful, but the stage was set. My dad didn't get sober until I was four years old. At that point, my parents had been fighting over his drinking for years. The alcoholic-codependent dance was something they knew well, and it didn't magically disappear the moment he started counting days in sobriety.

In our house, love is a regular topic of conversation. But there was something about the 1970s and the 1980s that made love a hands-off approach. Sure, walk down to the candy store by yourself. No big deal. I don't care if you wear shoes or not to the grocery store. Stay outside and don't come back until dark. We were a whole generation of self-sufficient kiddos, which became a whole generation of self-medicating adults.

We were the last real "children should be seen and not heard" generation in my family. My siblings and I were paid a quarter to stop whining, told to go outside and not come back until suppertime, and instructed to say, "Yes, ma'am," or "No, sir."

Our parents sent us to eat at the kids' table—scratch that—first, set the table and fill all the water glasses for the adults' table, and *then* go sit at the kids' table. My sister roared in the face of these duties and pleasantries, which often earned her a big, fat time-out in the hall, where she would roar by herself until it wore off. And let's not forget the spankings.

What did we learn here?

We learned that kids' needs were not as important as the adults'. We got the message that our need to express ourselves came second to adult family members' needs to be able to "hear themselves think." We learned that respect was a one-way street that only went in the direction of adults ("Yes, ma'am," "No, sir"), and that violence was justified if a parent deemed it necessary. We learned not to trust ourselves.

In this dynamic, it was a given that kids will get into trouble when left unsupervised. After all, we didn't have fully formed frontal lobes, nor anyone to ask for guidance in our neighborhood kid wilderness. I got my first cigarette on the school bus from a kid with a name like TJ, or JR, or something like that. I smoked it all by myself in the garage, where no one was looking for me because those were the times. I learned that I liked the way that it felt—both the drug and the sneaking. It gave me a sense of power, of agency that I didn't have while sequestered at the kids' table. The same would happen with my alcohol use.

We weren't invited to share about what was going on in our lives beyond our achievements. Many of us had overly strict or overly religious parents. And others had completely absent or neglectful parents. We saw the grown-ups of our generation smoking and drinking—the ads in magazines and on TV were promising how cool and glamorous life would be with booze and cigarettes. They even gave us candy cigarettes! When I was a kid in the 1980s and 1990s, it felt like everyone I knew had parents who were divorcing; there was this impending doom that any family trouble would result in divorce. So instead of learning to be full, whole, emotionally healthy people, we learned to self-medicate all of our fears and feelings bubbling under the surface.

We are a product of the generations that came before us. Both sets of my grandfathers fought in World War II, and their wives at home dealt with the impact of the Great Depression. My parents were products of a time filled with fear and scarcity and also the boom of technology that moved communities from being largely interconnected to being at home with the television and modern household appliances (washers, dryers, microwaves).

Not only did the generations that came before pass along their behaviors and beliefs, but there is research that shows trauma can alter a person's genes, and those genes are passed down through generations. But if trauma can be passed down, then perhaps so, too, can healing? I've often wondered how healing affects our genes. If we continue to move toward recovering our wholeheartedness in our families and in ourselves, there is a promise that we can recover the concepts of family for generations to come.

RECOVERING FAMILIES

On my first day as a teacher at our local middle school, I noticed the staff wearing T-shirts that had the word "Family" printed across the front. I felt a whoosh of spirit and belonging. I felt reassured because my mama was best friends with the social studies teacher's aunt, and my uncle went to high school with the technology teacher. I had walked into a community that believed we are *all* one family, and I felt an instant belonging.

Belonging to family means sharing a strong connection with the people in that family. Their experiences become our experiences. We develop a deepening in our empathy. Our family reflects back to ourselves, allowing us to build a stronger sense of who we are in the world while also recognizing the importance of connection.

We make true connections when we believe that we belong. I often joke that I don't do small talk; I go deep quickly, so prepare yourself for awkward if that's not what you're used to. Going deep together happens when there is a sense of connection. Connection is an energy. It's like Wi-Fi—when you're on a video call and you don't have a good connection, you only get half the message, or you appear frozen with your mouth open in the least flattering way.

"I'm here y'all! Can you hear me? Am I still frozen?"

When I'm not feeling connected with the people around me, I feel frozen and not fully heard. Sometimes all that's needed is to unplug for a minute and try again later. We could all use a good reset from time to time.

I know I belong when I don't have to hide any part of me. I can show up as I am to be a part of something bigger than me. I spent years of my life searching for belonging and instead found all the ways I didn't belong. One major obstacle to my sense of belonging was the inherent shame that came from not living true to myself, as Good Maggie or Bad Maggie (more on that soon). Later, the disconnect came from the fear of anyone knowing I was sober, or that I had a mental health history, or that I was vegetarian, or that I was a progressive liberal living in military communities in the South. For me, connection to others had to start with connecting to my values. When we live according to our values, regardless of what the masses are doing, we find people who share those same values, which cultivates connection.

Then, and this part can be tricky, we can bring those values home, even when they're not in alignment with those of our families of origin. It takes courage to actively live in a way that goes against the generational "curses" of those who came before us. If it is accessible, I believe it's possible to model what we are learning to our elders and become a beacon of healing in our biological families. If it is not accessible or healthy for us, then we can focus on modeling what we are learning for our chosen families. Both within and outside our biological families, healing begets healing.

Family is a two-way street of belonging and respect, even (and especially) for the youngest members. Being a part of a family means you are a part of something bigger than yourself. Being part of a family is honoring those who have gone before you, while carving out a new path ahead. It means that in my day-to-day life I honor and remember Jacob, my twin, and my grandparents who have passed, but I also honor myself and my children.

The more connection and healing we foster, the more we are able to see the humanity in all people, which brings us back to Dr. Martin Luther King Jr.'s quote at the beginning of this chapter. It stops being us versus them because it's actually ALL of us, in community. We must have the imagination to see our community fully restored. Because none of us are free until all of us are free.

When we allow *all* to be part of our family, our community, we can know the reconciliation and healing that comes with unconditional love and generosity of spirit—the modern-day barn raisings of transformation and collective recovery.

STEP ONE PRACTICE:
Your Family of Origin

The exercises in this book are meant to aid in your exploration through The 3 Things and your collective recovery.

In a journal that you'll use for each exercise, take a moment to answer each of these questions:

1. Who is your family of origin? What superpowers did you gain as a result of your origin family?

Are your superpowers still working?

EXAMPLE: *Worry can be a superpower that develops in early childhood because our brains are trying to keep us safe by covering all the bases and all the scenarios. Though it might have kept us protected at times, is it still working now?*

2. List all the good and not-so-helpful superpowers. Circle the ones that no longer serve you. Now, thank them for keeping you safe. Set an intention or say a prayer for the willingness to let go of any superpowers from your family of origin that aren't working for you.

EXAMPLE: *Thank you, worry, for keeping me safe through all of those scary nights. I'd like to try something different this time. Help me to stay in the moment rather than living in the past or worrying about the future. In this moment, I am okay.*

CHAPTER TWO

Rebuilding the Village

L ET ME KNOW IF YOU need anything!" The white notification box on my iPad lit up, interrupting my *Grey's Anatomy* binge.

My exhausted mom brain was overwhelmed thinking of something I needed and then actually asking for it. So, I ignored the message. Instead of reaching out for help, I reached over my nursing infant and hit play, diving back into the dramatic hospital scene on the screen.

"It takes a village to raise a child." This African proverb of unknown origin has been repeated exhaustively, in books and articles, on needlepoint pillows and bumper stickers, on social media and in Hallmark cards. We're quick to say, "It takes a village," and, "Let me know if you need anything."

But really, what village?

What do I *need*? I'll tell you what I need. I need to pee. I need an extra arm, or two. One of my barely four-week-old twins is nursing, the other is sleeping and they're going to switch places any minute. My boobs are sore and the left one is leaking every-where because they're so used to both babies eating at the same time. There is a mountain of laundry. My four-year-old is climbing the walls—and hasn't eaten anything but granola bars in seven weeks—and . . . Oh! Can't forget to put granola bars on the grocery list. Groceries! I really could use a shower. And a nap. But I'm starving. I could sleep in the shower while drinking a smoothie, maybe? I can't remember my last shower. Did I mention I have to pee? Where is my coffee mug? My husband only got two weeks of paternity leave and my family has gone home because their lives called them back.

Another text bubble came through. This time it read, "Let me know."

So, I replied, "We're doing great! If I need anything, I'll let you know!!! <3 xoxoxo!!! Heart emoji, heart emoji, kissy face emoji."

I turned back to *Grey's* and breastfeeding. It was the only thing I knew how to do.

I didn't need anything because I needed everything.

LEARNING HOW TO
CHOOSE YOUR FAMILY

One of my dear friends in college, during the party days, was CC. She was a rock, a lighthouse. While I was a chaotic and unstable party girl, she was consistent and reliable with good study habits and a stable home life. She loved me always and was there for me when I was wishy-washy and late for everything. We had children at similar ages, and I got to know her family during their time in school. Her oldest son, then age six (now a high school graduate), let us know that "There are no vampires allowed in this family." His adult self might be embarrassed to hear this story, but oh, how I smile thinking of it. What it means to me now is that we're allowed to kick out the proverbial bloodsuckers, those abusive narcissistic folks who steal our joy, energy, and resources. We don't need to compromise the entire village to keep their behaviors in the dark.

In modern society, no one knows more about suffering in silence than those of us who identify as moms. From the moment of birth, mothers are supposed to be supermoms, bearing the brunt of the physical labor of parenting and the invisible emotional labor of running a household. We do this, all while managing the expectations that go along with modern parenting, from babyproofing our houses to providing nutrition to picking out the perfect family Halloween costumes, and everything in between. There's this constant pull of Pinterest perfection pressure. And many moms do it all between forty hours a week of work or more.

"I don't know how you do it" is offered to us like a medal, weighing us down further as we drown in our individualism.

In some cultures, mothers aren't allowed to lift a finger other than to hold, feed, and bond with their new baby. The mothers and grandmothers and aunts surround the mother and feed and protect them so that they can heal and grow their new family. Years ago, in tribal times, mothers taught each other how to breastfeed (and even stepped in to breastfeed if a mother could not). All children were everyone's children. The village helped raise the children and mothers were honored; the load of managing a household was spread out among them.

The modern motherhood club has evolved from the old days of the village. There is an enormous amount of pressure on us to be and do it all when we know it's not humanly possible. We're expected to inherently know things without anyone teaching us. And then on top of it, we are pitted against one another.

Oh, the mommy wars on social media: fighting over breastfeeding versus bottle feeding, staying at home versus working, processed versus homemade food, vaccines versus anti-vax, and it goes on and on. Everything turns into a hard position and a rigid statement.

We put up walls and stand firm in our beliefs, rather than reaching around our walls to take care of one another and sharing vulnerably when we need help.

I get why we don't reach out for help. The expectations are so high, and the judgments can be devastating. And when we do finally ask for help, we're often given a list of all the ways we're doing it wrong rather than actually receiving loving help.

Sometimes, chosen family ends up replacing biological family if that family upholds hateful ideologies. Sometimes, politics isn't just a difference of opinion, but a matter of principle, of honoring the humanity of ALL and not just the ones under our roof, or those who look like us, are in our tax bracket, or in our country. Just the mention of politics used to make me very defensive. Today, I strive to use that defensive feeling as an opportunity to look into my own being and examine why I'm feeling that way. Am I being challenged to stretch? Am I afraid of losing something I have or not getting something I think I'm owed? This is a time to pause and say a mantra or a prayer.

"Lord, make me a channel of thy peace—that where there is hatred, I may bring love; that where there is wrong, I may bring the spirit of forgiveness; that where there is discord, I may bring harmony; that where there is error, I may bring truth; that where there is doubt, I may bring faith; that where there is despair, I may bring hope; that where there are shadows, I may bring light; that where there is sadness, I may bring joy. Lord, grant that I may seek rather to comfort than to be comforted— to understand, than to be understood; to love, than to be loved. For it is by self-forgetting that one finds. It is by forgiving that one is forgiven. It is by dying that one awakens to eternal life. Amen."

I still use the prayer of St. Francis to become aware of thought patterns and old ideas, grudges and resentments, and things that are blocking me from connection. It works every time.

RUGGED INDIVIDUALISM

The opposite of the village can be found in good old American individualism. From the beginning of our days (in Western society), we're urged to be self-sufficient and independent. I can count on one hand the number of times I've actually let anyone know if I needed anything. And even fewer times have people let me know when they were in need. "All by myself" is seen as a goal and a virtue, even as we're drowning in a sea of overwhelm.

Why can't we admit we need anything and everything? Why are we so fucking self-sufficient? We aren't wired this way as much as we try to be. We don't pop out of the womb ready to go the way some animals do. Mama snakes take off as soon as their eggs hatch. Some lizards and other reptiles don't even wait for the eggs to hatch, they just drop them and run. Harp seals leave their babies after only a few weeks, and rabbits leave their babies after only twenty-five days.

Can you imagine a human infant on its own at twenty-five months, much less weeks or days? We need family. We depend on them for survival. Throughout history, we've existed tribally, banding together in order to survive (it's the main reason we have survived for so long). One guy pulled down the branch while the other guy plucked the fruit, and they both ate. And later on, there was the butcher, the baker, and the candlestick maker (and the farmer and the seamstress, too). We are born relying on one another and we continue to survive because of this mutual reliance.

Once upon a time, all of the life-sustaining jobs happened on the farm or in the family. If you don't live in an extremely rural area, you can order most things with one click. I live in a pretty darn rural area and still I can get most anything in two days. Community is removed from the equation, and moms with newborns feel like the only thing to do is suffer in silence while binge-watching comfort shows. And ordering shit online.

If you've ever shared anything on social media that promotes the true meaning of the village, there's always at least one comment denouncing it as "socialism." It usually goes something like this:

> I've worked hard for everything I've gotten, it's my job to provide for my family, to suck it up and make it work even when it's hard. I provide for my family through good times and bad. I pulled myself up by my bootstraps; no one has ever handed me anything and I have struggled, and I made ends meet. I don't need help from anybody. You don't see me accepting handouts, and I turned out just fine. Stop spreading your socialist agenda.

The American dream is not what it used to be. Our parents' parents graduated high school and picked a job, they went to the college their parents could afford to pay for out-of-pocket. They got a job when they graduated college. There was one breadwinner who stayed in that forty-hour-a-week job and made enough money to support the entire family so mom could stay at home. And they stayed in the same neighborhood, their kids growing up together until they had their own kids.

Then everything got complicated. There's a job hiring somewhere in the Midwest a thousand miles from where I've always lived with my "village," but I'm willing to move because I need to keep up with this ever-elusive American dream of my parents. And the kids can't wait to grow up and move out of the house. So, they move as soon as they can, and go to college and take out lots of loans, but there aren't any jobs so they work in whatever job they can get and spend decades paying back the loans. And we're all just so busy making ends meet that there is no time to be a community.

For a while, the Army had a recruiting ad that said, "Army of one." Not surprising, as a lot of military members and supporters espouse this idea, this myth of rugged individualism. The fires of this idea are stoked to keep us alone, to make us forget about the village, but the military couldn't be less for the individual if it tried. Slogans that are drilled into our heads from day one of boot camp—"One team, one fight," "Mission first," "People always," "Loose lips sink ships"—stress the importance of conforming to community standards. My husband's boot camp platoon slogan was "One heart, one blood, one soul." "Semper Fidelis" (always faithful), is the Marine Corps motto. They talk about an army of one, but the truth is, the military instills that we are all one, working together in perfect community.

When we were stationed at Camp Lejeune, in Jacksonville, North Carolina, we had our first "Friendsgiving." It was 2009, and my husband and I weren't married yet. We were celebrating Thanksgiving away from our families, in our new duty station, before having our first child with each other. We came together at our friend JD's house, each with our own traditional family recipes, sharing laughs and funny stories. JD opened with the most awkward prayer where he deemed us the wolf pack forever as we stood circled around our feast table, holding hands. We were a group of five mostly non-religious Marines and their spouses. Twelve years later, we're all still friends, just with more gray hair or less hair, all with larger families and spread all over the United States.

What we found in the veteran communities wasn't rugged individualism or a bootstrapping mentality, we found friendship and camaraderie. We found people who would stick by us through thick and thin. We found family, a community of strangers who, despite their diverse backgrounds and differing lived experiences, all shared a common bond. JD was right, we were a wolf pack. And like wolves, though we know how to survive on our own, we have learned that it's more fun to share food and howl at the moon together.

HOW TO MAKE OUR FAMILY
FUNCTION AS A VILLAGE

Whether we like it or not, humans are motivated by pain. The desire to be a part of a community often goes unnoticed until we are suffering. In my case, I would only reach out during times of hard newborns, illness, grieving, or a pain so great, a suffering so intense that I had no other choice. But how can we build a true village if we only reach out when our hut is on fire? I have to be honest with myself and my people about what I need because otherwise, it will be too late by the time I've sent distress signals. And don't get me wrong, they're there—fights with my partner, fussy kids, unmanageable housework—and when I try to do it all myself during these times, I usually end up in bed sick to the point where I *have* to call in reinforcements for basic survival.

WHY ARE WE LIKE THIS?

The irony is, in learning how to ask for what we need, we give others permission to be human and accept help too. We begin to recover together.

When you see people in a twelve-step program portraying the first step in movies or books, often they say something like, "The first step is admitting that you have a problem." The first step to fixing any problem is having an awareness of it. But here's what the first step actually says, "We admitted we were powerless over alcohol and that our lives had become unmanageable." Focus on the words "we" and "our." I never really noticed them in the early days of sobriety until I heard an old-timer (that's what we call folks in twelve-step rooms that have been sober for a while) share that it's a "we" program. All twelve steps are worded this way to illustrate that we are part of a community.

For my parents, their chosen family was the church community, and that may work for some. But studies have shown that more and more young people are moving away from the church. It may be because of the same things I discussed previously in this chapter (supermom myth, individualism, the end of the American dream, the great busy). Maybe we just don't have the time or energy to go to church. Or maybe, and more likely, we're disenchanted with religion and the mixed messaging we hear from our disparate belief systems.

But that doesn't change our need for chosen family.

If you're my age or older you remember the TV show *Cheers*. The opening song goes like this, "Sometimes you wanna go / Where everybody knows your name / And they're always glad you came / You wanna go where you can see / Our troubles are all the same / You wanna go where everybody knows your name."

When I first joined the Navy, my chosen family was my fellow nuke school buddies (Nuclear Power Training) and on the ship, the nukes stuck together. We were in the trenches with long hours and stressful work conditions, and if I'm honest, we were a bit weird. The key for me was finding my weirdos, and the same was true with my nursing school friends later on. My drinking buddies in my favorite bars were like the *Cheers* friends on TV. For several years, I always had a spot where I walked in, and everyone yelled "Maggie!" just like the characters yelled "Norm!" from the original show. I could always count on two Michelob Ultras in front of my spot at the bar.

Another chosen family over the years was my running family. After my middle child was born, I wanted to lose weight and I didn't know how because I had a child with me everywhere I went. I learned about this invention called the jogging stroller. I found a used one on Craigslist and a beginner app and soon fell in love with the sport. I found other moms with strollers on Facebook, and we started meeting and running together; it turns out that there are all kinds of running clubs for all kinds of people. When I ran alone, I felt like everyone was looking at me from behind window blinds, saying mean things like, "She thinks she's running," and, "Yeah, she needs to run." Finding my running friends made me feel like I was allowed to run; it gave me permission to show up, whatever my size or mood, because they were showing up too. We commiserated over parenting woes and traded running tips to make it all more bearable and fun.

The moms in my first running club are still my chosen family. And running is still one of my favorite things to do when my health allows, even though I've ditched the idea of changing my body weight on purpose. One of my first plans of action when we hit a new duty station is connecting with the local running groups in the area. I do the same with the military spouse groups and recovery communities. This is how I cultivate my chosen family in any town. It's all about finding my fellow weirdos.

I was waiting on my flight home in the Baltimore airport recently when a Marine approached me and shook my hand. He assumed I was military because of my short haircut. A bit of small talk revealed that he was a gunnery sergeant stranded at the airport, having just arrived stateside from deployment in Afghanistan. He was locked out of his car and was trying to pay a locksmith. All I had to hear was that he was a gunny, home from deployment. Without hesitation, I gave him enough cash to pay the locksmith and feed himself for the day.

Sure, I may have gotten scammed, but if he was willing to invoke Semper Fi to scam me, that's on him. I did my part by helping from the heart. We find our chosen family in all areas of our life—it's the "I got you, babe" mentality that makes it less scary to reach out our hands and ask for help. And it makes it easier for us to reach out and help someone else.

We don't have to be "an Army of One," despite the advertising. We are not meant to be solitary beings. When we find our chosen family and deem them our favorite bunch of weirdos, we can build each other up. We can ask for help when we don't know what to do next. We can share our experience, teach each other what's worked for us, and hold space when nothing else will. We can have each other's back, whether on the battlefield (or on watch in the engine room) or whether we're pushing an insanely heavy double stroller around our neighborhoods.

We're organizing ourselves by all the things we are against, rather than by all the things we support. We pretend we are superheroes and rugged individuals and that we don't need help.

> We sit alone in our cape, always willing to save, but not willing to be saved.

To build collective recovery, we have to let go of this old American dream and reimagine a reality that embraces everyone instead of praising the individual.

We often have lived experiences or trauma that take the idea of belonging away from us. The great marketing campaign of society has led us to believe that in order to belong we must be thinner, richer, more successful, always positive, perfect, etc. But the fact is, we belong because we exist. There is nothing wrong with us, and there never was.

We turn inward to our families, to find deeper connections as a result of the pain and because we want to do better and be better. We want better for our kids just like our parents wanted better for us than they had. We all have it within us to find this chosen family or to turn to our families of origin.

We have to imagine systems where we aren't competing or depending on charity but where everyone is seen for the dignity that they possess as humans. We have to imagine a world where we aren't trying to decide who deserves what. Because we are all deserving.

In 1996, "Because You Loved Me" by Celine Dion topped the charts. I learned the song, both vocally and in sign language, and performed it for my parents. Our love wasn't perfect, but it made me what I am. They are the first family I became a part of. When I was born, I didn't have to do anything to deserve that love. My parents gave that love to me because I was theirs.

Daddy once said to me, "Sometimes I'm still not sure you're going to survive, but you keep on proving me wrong." This honest admission of the pain of my birth and his witness to the events of my life since pushed my "I don't belong" button at first. I survived premature birth, severe illness as a young child, military life, divorce, alcoholism, suicide, a car accident, long COVID, a brain tumor—each survival, a measure of how much I DO belong. The message I get to share is that I belong because I exist. You belong because you exist. And when we acknowledge each other's humanity by existing together in community, we are part of a family.

STEP TWO PRACTICE:
Your Human Family

What can you do right now to see that you belong in our human family? Start noticing your neighbors. Really see the passengers on the bus, the subway, or the airplane. Make eye contact. Smile. Witness. Give honest compliments. Do random acts of kindness. Notice the angry folks. Acknowledge the fear on the faces of the people who are pulled over in a traffic stop. See the faces of people as you're driving.

What is the experience of people in your community? Are the people around you happy? Hurting? Content? Hungry? Anxious? Calm?

Take in the scowls or the bobbing heads of your fellow commuters on the way to work. Hold space for the woman struggling at the checkout with her screaming kids. Is she worried that her card may not go through or embarrassed about the number of coupons?

Maybe you don't have to change anything about your behavior, just notice. Open your eyes to the world around you. Take mental notes of our common humanity. When you let in the faces and eyes and smiles around you, you may find that there is more of a village than you once thought. You may discover that the doom and gloom of the news reports and the calls to be hypervigilant don't feel quite right. Notice the humanity. Notice your village. It never left.

CHAPTER THREE

The Undeniable Miracle of Human Connection

Thank all that is good for my moment and gift of desperation when I told Tony the therapist that I had tried and failed at my own suicide the night before. His office had wood paneling, the décor included faded mass-produced prints and a clock of wood and brass. The only inviting part of the room was the man himself, gently asking questions to pull secrets out of me that were keeping me sick and stuck. The part of me that wanted to die sat watching the part of me that wanted to live give up the whole jig. I was exposed and terrified, and somehow relieved. That was the moment my recovery truly began.

My first sponsor in my recovery from alcoholism always said, "This disease wants us dead, but it will take us drunk and alone too." This is true of all of the "isms" and "dis-ease" that are ever present in our modern culture. When I am isolated and alone, I'm left to believe everything that goes on between my ears. I become afraid of the dark, and I start to believe everything I read on the internet. This path of isolation and addiction led me to believe it would be better for me to take my own life than face what lingered in the vast darkness that I feared so much.

If family is a series of concentric circles, the smallest one would be my own core humanity. The next circle includes those who live under my roof. The next circle is parents and siblings, then comes my cousins and nieces and nephews and friends who are like family, then my workplace, then local town and state and region, and on and on. These circles go on until there's a big ol' earth-sized circle that includes all of humanity and sentient beings that our lives help or harm.

Since we're all inherently the center of our own universe, and our concentric circles, it's important to also become aware that our circles intersect with others' circles. Our actions (or inactions) create ripples, and those ripples make ripples. We are interconnected. We may perceive that we are separate, different, and that our lives have nothing to do with each other. But the truth is, we are part of something bigger than ourselves. Having a circle that tells us, "You belong because you are you," and, "You belong because you exist," helps override the voices that tell us we aren't enough or that we have to do it alone, all by ourselves, harder, better, faster, stronger. Our conditioning tells us they won't like us anymore if we appear as imperfect people with human needs and if we admit we can't do it all by ourselves.

But we are all imperfect people with human needs, the biggest need being each other.

There is risk in looking up and out of our inner circle. It makes us vulnerable. If you see who I really am, will you love me? Will you judge me for my messy humanness? But in order to build social capital—the respect and trust that holds our communities and families together—we must become vulnerable, even when the lion is chasing us, even when we're the lion.

CONNECTION CREATES COMMUNITY

There is no isolation like rock bottom. Our obsession with self-sufficiency, and in turn, the decline in social capital, has made it nearly impossible to cope. We're attempting to meet needs that can't be met alone, no matter how hard we try. Instead of asking for help, we turn to comforts and coping tools, or self-medication. We try our best to fill the hole in our soul that feels bigger and emptier in the dark all by ourselves. This may come in the form of alcohol, food, spending, drugs, sex, gambling, overwork, doomscrolling on social media, or excessive exercise. I can use anything, good or bad, to the extreme until it no longer works, and I'm left with that hole again, which has only become wider and deeper due to the guilt, shame, and remorse for over-whatever-ing.

Connection creates community by increasing our social capital. "Social capital" is a science-y term to describe this idea of connectedness, the resources of respect and trust that are engendered among networks and involvement among groups of people. You find social capital wherever you find people working or playing together. More social capital means more tight-knit but also healthier and safer communities. It is the community glue.

In our community of concentric circles with each individual at the center, we are the center of our own universes. But when we are in our primitive survival state of fight or flight, it's hard to look up and see how far out the circles of community go. Who gives a shit about connection when we're running from a lion? While we're not literally being chased by lions anymore, our brains are still wired to protect us in times of danger. When we are in self-protection mode, we become extremely short-sighted. The problem is we find ourselves in an almost constant state of self-protection.

> The true gifts lie beyond that shortsightedness when we move from self-protection to connection.

When we connect with each other in an authentic way, we are rewarded with the reassurance that we are not alone. The "I thought I was the only one" isolation illusion is blown open. You can't have an open bag of chips in the house without them disappearing too? I thought I was the only one! You walk into a room and completely forget what you were doing and just stare at the wall for several minutes trying to remember? I thought I was the only one! You're afraid someone is going to find out you have no idea what you're doing? I thought I was the only one! You feel like you're failing at parenthood or life in general? I thought I was the only one!

When I am stuck in myself, I am in the prison of my own damn drama Hula-Hoop. Only after being pulled into the fold can we find that freedom of recovery. We are free to be ourselves, which allows others the freedom to be themselves.

Remember, none of us is free until we're all free. Connection gives us an opening to be honest and authentic in our suffering and to seek out those who have been where we are and have found a solution.

Every time I enter a twelve-step recovery room, I am given the gift of connection. I'm in a room of fellow survivors of a common peril, bonding over drunk logs and a collective solution. Many of us feel seen for the first time ever when we enter recovery rooms. This common bond that we share and the scaffolding to have safe conversations and connections gives some of us the first glimpse of what it means to say, "You are part of a family."

We tend to forget that suffering is something that we all go through. When we are hurting, it's easy to turn inward and keep everything to ourselves, but that keeps us from looking up and outward to see that we aren't alone in our suffering. It's only when we look up that we can see that there is a solution. An old proverb says, "A problem shared is a problem halved. A joy shared is a joy doubled."

CONVERSATION CREATES COMMUNITY

For me, summer is sticky hands and stale angel food cake, covered in boiled sugar icing and strawberries, that my grandmama made for my June birthday. The grown-ups would leave it out for everyone to walk by and tear off a piece whenever they wanted, and I loved when it got slightly stale. Food is a big part of most of my childhood memories. I can't hear an ice cream truck without thinking of orange sherbet Push Pops and sticky hands. There's something about food that evokes some of the strongest connections.

When we were stationed in Monterey, California, our duplex shared a wall with a neighboring family from Pakistan. Jamil and his wife and daughters were there for a short while, but I wanted to make sure they felt at home in America. I activated my southern roots and baked for them (I studied the dietary practices for their religion to make sure I wasn't going to offend). I shared a big batch of vegetarian chili and cornbread muffins. The day after I sent over the dish, there was a knock at our door, and one of their daughters gifted us a warm plate of pakora (a South Asian version of vegetable fritters)! Jamil's wife did not speak English and I don't speak Urdu, but sharing our dishes and cultures with one another was our way of speaking from the heart. I sent over cookies and brownies, and she sent back all sorts of traditional Pakistani dishes. We would include little notes with our dishes, doing our best to Google Translate for the other. These were the extent of our conversations. We never broke bread in person, but I deeply loved that family. It was an adventure of food and love for me, a way to communicate beyond words; I hope Jamil's family felt the same way.

Food provides the perfect opportunity for conversation across barriers. What kinds of conversations can we have while breaking bread? We've all been told not to talk politics at the dinner table. It's just not comfortable, right? For too long, the powers-that-be have depended on us to keep the peace in our families and communities and to stay out of politics. We've been taught to leave it to the politicians and the stakeholders, and now none of us know how to civically engage in conversation, nor is civic engagement even common knowledge. Do you know who your elected officials are? Do you know what the issues and problems of your community are?

> The thing about privilege is that things are only problems when they start to affect us personally.

It's time we widen our perspective and our knowledge of how we are being governed and take an active role in the process so that our biggest family gets the care that we all deserve as humans. All of this starts with conversation, and some warm cornbread sure wouldn't hurt either.

In today's highly polarized and divided social climate, we've forgotten how to interact kindly with all types of people. Robert George and Cornell West are on opposite sides of the political spectrum, conservative and progressive respectively. Yet they have found a way to go beyond their defensiveness to have civil discourse and, dare I say, a deep friendship. Their work involves touring and speaking about this idea. In "Resurrecting Civil Discourse: In Conversation with Robert George and Cornel West," they write, "A painfully divided America can return to civil discourse only if people on all sides of the civic divide make themselves vulnerable to being challenged on their convictions, adopt the humility that they might be wrong, and respect the humanity of those who disagree with them." All of this starts with conversation.

How can we be vulnerable, humble, and respectful during civil discourse? It can be really hard to remember we're all connected when every scroll on social media shows comment sections full of ALL CAPS arguing and where no one is willing to listen or be wrong. We could start by removing the anonymity of the screen and sit down at the dinner table together to share our stories. We can connect by learning about each other, who we are and where we came from, what we like to do for fun, and what food we grew up eating.

West gives this advice on how to connect with those who aren't interested in civil discourse: "Ask them about their mama. Ask them about their child. Ask them about sports. It lets people know you don't come in with arrogance and condescension. It acknowledges, 'This is who I am. This is who you are. Let's see what small overlap we might find.'" When we engage in this way, we see all the ways we are connected, rather than disconnected.

STEPPING OUTSIDE OF PRIVILEGE AND INTO COMMUNITY

As a white woman raised in the South, I had the privilege of being able to stay apolitical most of my life. For a very long time, I said, "I don't do politics." For a decade, all I did was vote and watch the presidential debates. That was the extent of my civic duties. And then one afternoon, I saw a story about Tamir Rice on my social media feed. He was twelve years old and playing with a toy gun in his yard when he was murdered by police. My child was only a year older than Tamir was at the time of his murder. I watched my son happily playing in our yard, and it brought me to my knees with grief. The footage of

Philando Castile being executed in his car in 2016 hit me in a similar way.

But like a lot of white ladies, my grief ended there. I was shocked and sad, but what was I supposed to do about it? It wasn't until Trump was elected that I hit the ground running, cramming in all the action I had ignored in my adult years. I was furious and busy, attending group after group, meeting after meeting. At some point in 2019, after daily bombshells exploding on the newsfeeds and threats to so many, I became jaded at all the talking sessions, all the meetings where different (but mostly white) groups were saying the same things over and over and doing nothing.

I was lonely living in military communities where the right-leaning folks were loud and proud, and the left-leaning folks were unknown to me. When we moved to California in 2018, I was hoping I could out myself as liberal right away and find my people (because y'all remember how divided and isolating things were then). But after the first few meetups with my favorite military running group (even in California), I decided I would stay politically anonymous, and I would work privately on becoming more aware and civically engaged.

Five weeks into our next duty station move, we were hit by a national pandemic and the world stopped. We were happily hunkered down in our pandemic bubble, masking in public and going contact-free. I never in a gazillion years could have imagined a public health emergency becoming so politicized! The mask debate was mind-boggling and my new friends became distant acquaintances after I watched them continue to go out and have large gatherings despite the recommendations against such activities. When Ahmaud Arbery's murder in Georgia came to the attention of the media, followed by George Floyd's murder, I was done with being alone and isolated. I needed to find the people who were taking real action so I could learn how to be an active member of my largest family, my humanity family. We moved to Georgia, where I joined a fledgling grassroots organization called SOWEGA Rising.

I was finally part of a group that shared my interest in taking action for change in southern Georgia. I stepped out of my privilege and stepped into the service of my community. I showed up to events, setting up chairs and carrying signs, and I even got to speak at a march. I've continued to show up, and I'm so honored to say that our fledgling group is now a thriving nonprofit where I am proud to serve as a board member.

All of our choices matter, not just our choices at the polls. Where we're spending our money, whether or not we're getting vaccinated and wearing masks during a global pandemic, whether we amplify love and connection or hatred and violence, our choices either move us toward the selfish individual or toward the loving family/village mindset. When I make my choices, I ask myself: "Am I being true to myself? Am I glorifying God with this choice? Am I honoring my greater human family?"

My prayer is that we see our modern times as an opportunity for us to turn to one another as our biggest and greatest family, to glorify God by acknowledging the dignity and humanity in one another. As bell hooks once wrote, "Beloved community is formed not by the eradication of difference but by its affirmation, by each of us claiming the identities and cultural legacies that shape who we are and how we live in the world."

When we show up in community being true to ourselves, we have the chance to be celebrated by what makes us unique, while simultaneously celebrating the differences of others.

There are many who can't wait to get out of town when they grow up. They pine for something bigger and better than their childhood beginnings. I remember desperately wanting to move to a city, far away from my small town. We did move to South Florida during my sophomore year in high school, and I am so glad that I did. I was exposed to a wide range of different cultures. But you know what I'm also really glad for? Moving back to my hometown where I am now teaching middle school in southern Georgia (in the town where I was born). I wish that more folks would either stay or come back. Maybe it's the wisdom of getting older or the need to slow down after decades of being busy, but the gift of community is proving to be my favorite part of being home.

Investing in social capital, building relationships, and showing up for your community makes a difference. Extraordinary things happen when ordinary people come together for a common cause. We change our own personal outlook and learn compassion and empathy. We feel a sense of purpose that comes from being a part of something bigger than ourselves. We make movements by bridging our values with political activism and change. We boost morale of our neighborhoods by learning to have fun together again as a family.

And as we show up for our community, our largest family, learning to love and live our authentic selves, we get to experience a power greater than ourselves. Some of us call that power God or a Higher Power, or as I like to call it, HP. Some call it intuition or love or their home group. We come to believe that a power greater than ourselves is working in our lives.

Belief plus evidence over time equals faith.

Together we can effect change, loving one another more, celebrating our humanity, and recovering together. When we realize we're no longer alone, we have access to a new hope that gives way to faith in something bigger than ourselves. That hope makes room for change to come in, for a solution, for a new plan to emerge and take hold. We can learn from others how to live authentically true to ourselves.

All of this opens us up to honoring the humanity in each of us. We are part of a family.

STEP THREE PRACTICE:
Your Circles of Community

This connection practice is a loving-kindness meditation. The goal of this type of meditation is to cultivate connection and kindness toward all beings, our largest family.

Start by sitting in a comfortable position. Close your eyes. Take a slow, deep breath in through your nose and continue breathing deeply. *In your mind's eye, see yourself sitting in a beautiful Hula-Hoop.* It may be golden, or your favorite color, but it is a magic Hula-Hoop that makes you feel joyful, safe, and peaceful, just by sitting inside the circle.

While still imagining your beautiful Hula-Hoop, feel your breath traveling through your body. Notice your heart space. Imagine there is a golden thread that moves from your heart space and surrounds you just like your Hula-Hoop; it may even become your Hula-Hoop if you wish.

Say this phrase, directing it to yourself:

"May I know joy, May I be safe, May I know peace."

Slowly repeat: *"May I know joy, May I be safe, May I know peace."*

Think about what these words mean and how they make you feel. If you start to get distracted or feel silly, say to yourself, "It's okay," and continue with the phrase.

Now, allow your heart-thread Hula-Hoop to grow until it encompasses the people you consider family. You can think about a specific person or a group of people. Recite the phrase toward them:

"May you know joy. May you be safe. May you know peace."
Again, recognize the meaning and how you feel.

Now, allow your circle to grow. Include everyone in your community, making sure to include those you find difficult.

"May you know joy. May you be safe. May you know peace."
Again, recognize the meaning and acknowledge how you're feeling, even if your feelings are negative. Imagine that a golden light is shining from your heart-thread Hula-Hoop and light is passing over everyone in your community. Repeat the phrase until you experience compassionate feelings. Do a final round to make your Hula-Hoop expand to *all* creation.

"May you know joy. May you be safe. May you know peace."

CHAPTER FOUR

Humanity Is a Good Thing (I Promise)

Just before noon on a Friday in late March 2021, an elderly woman was walking along West Forty-Third Street in New York City on her way to church, when an assailant yelled, "F— you, you don't belong here!" and began beating her within inches of her life. He singled her out and attacked her because she was Asian. And across the nation, hate crimes against the Asian community had been skyrocketing after the Trump administration encouraged anti-Asian sentiment with its handling of the coronavirus pandemic. As if this weren't horrific enough, there were witnesses, bystanders who watched and did nothing while this woman was beaten. Video surveillance of the crime showed that at least three men witnessed the assault and did nothing. This is what happens when we "draw the circle of family too small" as Mother Teresa once said.

> When we don't honor each other as family, we stop standing up for one another. And we lose our own humanity.

Our future depends on us being part of a family. If we do not start seeing each other as a family, as common humanity, we are going to rip each other apart. Already we are seeing the dehumanization of entire groups of people—Asian, immigrant, Black, Brown, Indigenous, and LGBTQIA+ people. This is not new, it's happened throughout our history, but today, there is a resurgence with a boldness to it. With this dehumanizing language and the actions/inaction of our communities, the uptick in hate-related violence and mass shootings will only increase. The legislation against human rights will only continue.

Our future depends on us being a family. This means honoring all members of our family just as they are, not arguing about their right to exist. We are no longer going to debate whether trans people should have rights (because they do). We are no longer going to debate about gender expression and identity because there is an entire spectrum of existence that is supported by science. We are no longer going to question whether or not Black, Brown, and Indigenous people face racism. Of course they do.

What we are going to do, as members of this human family, is take courageous action to face it and stop it. We're going to honestly acknowledge the world as it is, so we can imagine the world as it could be. Oh, that place is a world where we all have enough to eat, where we all belong and share equal human rights, where all members of our greater family feel safe. Where bad players are held accountable, and greed is not rewarded. Where creativity is encouraged, and critical thinking is taught. I see a future where family is the building block for this, with blood relatives and community coming together to build this one new, beloved family.

BUILDING BELOVED CHILDREN

I've loved butterflies for as long as I can remember. Some might say I'm obsessed—they've inspired my tattoos, my classroom decor, and my yelps of glee when I see one in the wild. I get the question from my students all the time, "What's with the butterfly thing?"

My response? The butterfly thing is an outward reminder of hope, that in our darkest times we can hold on to the fact that we will emerge, and we will fly. Their chrysalises show us that we can surround and nurture one another so we all have the opportunity to grow our wings.

A coworker and my son's chorus teacher, Debbie Hamlin, gave me the following analogy for our students. Primary school children are like little caterpillars, happily moving along, hungry and gobbling up everything in their path. Middle schoolers, however, undergo a complete transformation. They come in as little caterpillars, and they have no idea what is about to hit them. They shed their skin and go inward, into their cocoon where it's dark and gooey and you just have to hope they're okay in there. And then, just when you think they'll never come out, they emerge as butterflies with beautiful wings, ready, or nearly ready, to fly. Now, if we try to force those kiddos out of the cocoon too soon, their wings won't be as strong. We need to give them the space and time to grow. With society the way it is today, some get ripped out too early by life, so we as teachers and trusted grown-ups have to encircle them and be their cocoon until it's safe for them to stand and fly on their own.

In my first year of teaching, I had several kids in my classroom who challenged my patience. Their behavior left me scrambling to actually teach. I spent a whole lot of time redirecting behavior. My nervous system would get all worked up and I'd want to blame all the hard things about teaching on them. They joked that Mrs. Boxey uses her military voice too much. I'd much rather be a sweet southern peach than a drill sergeant, but dang it, it's hard! (Military life has prepared me well for teaching middle school, I tell you what.)

Hats off to veteran teachers—until you've lived it, there is no way to know how hard this job is. In my desperation to make an impact on this generation of children whose attention spans are no longer than fifteen-second TikTok clips and who are two to three years behind due to a pandemic, I attended a seminar by Amie Dean, the Behavior Queen. I wish every adult could sit in on one of her seminars. She led with a quote by Ashleigh Warner, "Beneath every behavior there is a feeling. And beneath every feeling there is a need. And when we meet that need rather than focus on the behavior, we begin to deal with the cause, not the symptom."

When I heard that, I realized I needed to find the cause in my students, rather than the symptoms.

The truth is, many of the children I teach have experienced unimaginable trauma. And that's not even including chronic hunger or the collective trauma of a global pandemic. There is no time to genuinely reach each child where they are, meeting their needs and honoring their trauma, when our funding depends on test scores and teachers are working second jobs to pay their bills.

If every child in every area had access to a wholehearted education, with their humanity being boosted and their core values protected, we would see an increase in the health and happiness of our communities. We would have less violence and hate and heartache; instead, we would see more butterflies.

BUILDING A BELOVED SOCIETY

When we are living as if we are part of a family, the community's needs matter. When we are living as if we are part of a family, we want to see our family members healthy and happy, fed and living their own personal definition of success. Unfortunately, our individualistic views and our unbendable concentric circles make us view those outside our front door as "the others." Othering keeps us from living together in community and steals the humanity from us all.

To have a healthy family (world), we have to embrace change, invite it in, and open our eyes to the fact that what we've been doing isn't working. We have to see that even though we may be comfortable in our station, our choices may be having a negative impact on other members of our beloved family. We have to see that welcoming even the smallest changes can make a difference in the lives of our biggest human family. Changes in our attitudes and behavior today lead to systemic changes that benefit us all. We can call for educational, religious, and judicial change, standing up for those who need our help, and against violence and racism when we watch it taking place in front of us.

While politicians figure out ways to entice their followers with privatization of education, after decades of decreased funding to public education, we teachers are on the front lines trying to make do with what we have. It's odd thinking of teaching as being on the front lines, but we are battling more than anyone on the outside knows. My kids have been trained on what to do if an active shooter comes into our school, while access to the arts has all but dwindled (shout out to the art, chorus, and band teachers!), and recess is a thing of the past.* We've sacrificed creativity and play for scarcity and vigilance. That's not a great environment for nurturing young minds. The goalposts have moved from raising future community members and helping children develop mentally and socially, to how can we get our test scores higher. The child is lost in the mix, just a number, or worse, another casualty.

True support of public education across the country begins in the communities. Those community members who vote down education taxes and funding are clipping the butterfly wings of the human beings who will care for us in the future.

Since 2002, the *World Happiness Report* has used statistical analysis to determine the world's happiest countries. Researchers analyze countries' happiness by monitoring performance in six particular categories: gross domestic product per capita, social

---

* I am proud to say that since I first typed this, our school has implemented a Friday break where our kids get an hour outside to play. I am proud to be a part of a school system that is doing its best to do more than just raise test scores, even in the face of ever-dwindling funding.

support, healthy life expectancy, freedom to make your own life choices, generosity of the general population, and perceptions of internal and external corruption levels. In a 2021 *World Happiness Report*, the United States scored nineteenth on the list. What do the happiest countries have that the United States doesn't have? Finland, the happiest country in that 2021 study, showed "strong feelings of communal support and mutual trust" and "that they were free to make their own choices, and showed minimal suspicion of government corruption."

The seven top-scoring countries, all in Northern Europe, have high levels of community generosity, social support (universal healthcare and schools and housing programs), and a general sense of safety with little to no perceived corruption in their local and national governing bodies.

As Whitney Houston once wisely sang, children are the future. Those measures of happiness? They affect our children. Every child should be seen as a whole human being with a future, wants, needs, and challenges just like you and me, not a test score or statistic. They can't live in their full humanity if they are hungry, houseless, or sick. They can't learn if they are worried about active shooters coming into their school. They can't live their full humanity if funding for schools is stripped to the bare minimum and a fair opportunity for quality education and social support isn't provided.

But school isn't the only place where we can build collective recovery.

If all churches were like Daddy's, this might be a much more religious-centric little book. As he grew and evolved as a minister, I saw our church family grow and evolve. He learned Spanish in order to perform services for the neighborhood Spanish-speaking community. He reminded our church family often that ALL were invited and that if you were in our church, you were home. He blessed same-sex marriages long before the church or the state recognized them. He delighted in how multicultural our church family became, and when he made a misstep, he did his best to correct it. I watch him now, learning to be anti-racist, unlearning his own upbringing, and carrying the message as he believes that Jesus intended, table flipping and all.

BUILDING BELOVED HUMANITY

As we evolve as a society, we must make room for everyone at the table. Religious reform must be progressive, not regressive, and if it doesn't include all as our beloved family, then it's not of love. The presiding bishop of the Episcopal Church in the United States has a sermon entitled "If It's Not About Love, It's Not About God." We can't be loving if we're busy banning books and drag shows and the human right to safe and critical reproductive healthcare.

When brutality is the norm, humanity is lost. And we're not just talking about the institutions of school and church, but also the state. From the policing system, through the courts, on to the prison for profit, the entire justice system needs to be reworked. Police officers are called when people are at their worst moments and for what? Why is a person with a gun and a Taser and a baton showing up to a mental health crisis? We can do our part by not calling the police for noise complaints and mental health crises. We can be better humans by acknowledging the humanity in all, by letting those around us exist, by pausing when agitated and asking ourselves if there is a real danger from someone who is different from us, or if it's our conditioning that made us feel there is danger.

When we were stationed in Monterey, we loved to go walking along the Old Fisherman's Wharf and Cannery Row as a family—especially at Christmastime. With my southeastern upbringing I always pictured California as perpetually sunny and warm, but Monterey is cool and overcast much of the year—and freezing on a windy pier during late December. There is a very large community of folks facing houselessness in this area, and it wasn't at all odd to see many people hunkered down along the wharf trail, as city ordinances and anti-homeless legislation turned them into outcasts. On one particular day of Christmas lights and sightseeing, I noticed a woman who appeared to live on the street with her dog and her few belongings. I noticed, but I passed on by with my subconscious need to avert my gaze and keep it moving.

My child, Clayton, and the twins did not keep it moving. "Your dog is so cute!" one of them told her. "How are you today? We're getting hot cocoa and seeing Santa Claus and maybe getting candy, right, Mom?" The joy of connection flooded the woman's face, and I felt ashamed for wanting to pass by without acknowledging her. When I looked closer, I could see that she had gorgeous eyes and deep smile lines. The kids continued talking with her unabashedly and cheerfully petting her pup (after asking for permission, we don't go touching animals without permission, kiddos). We eventually said our goodbyes and continued to walk down the wharf through the bustle of shopping and lights. When it was time to get our hot cocoa, the kids got together and decided that we needed to get our new friend some, as well as a cup of clam chowder that was so popular on this strip. They returned to her with their warm gifts and eagerly picked back up with the conversation and reports of the fun had since our last meeting.

I quietly placed a bill in the cup next to her sign asking for help. Clayton saw this and dug deep in their pockets for change from the souvenir they bought moments before. "Thank you for your kindness," the woman said with a smile. "It's rare these days."

But it doesn't have to be.

Another wave of shame washed over me as I remembered all the times I ignored or outright avoided similar situations. Honoring her humanity (my kids didn't hesitate at this) was what all of us needed that evening, maybe me most of all.

> If we continue to see those outside our front door as others, with lives and circumstances that don't concern us, then we will lose all sight of humanity.

We'll see history repeated, and whole groups of people will (continue to) be targeted. Dangerous legislation, permitting the continued unchecked self-interest of the few, will keep getting pushed through against the will of the majority and against our democracy. The gap between the haves and have-nots will grow and all the symptoms of corruption and dis-ease will get worse. Those who gain power from our division will tell us to blame our neighbor, those in need, or the opposing political party supporters. They'll say it's because we're not living green enough while dumping tons of toxins in the air and water. They'll convince us that it's the generation before or after us ruining everything. We'll grow angrier, more afraid, and sicker, while they rake in the profits from our delusion that we are separate.

This human family is the only family we have. We honor that family by acknowledging that each one of us has infinite value, not because of how much good they do or how hard they work or what they produce, but because they exist. This idea must inform how we treat others, whether it's our friends or neighbors, our students or our teachers, strangers, travelers, refugees, disabled people, addicts, shut-ins, or the guy who hangs out at the entrance to the grocery store asking for spare change. All human beings are worthy of dignity and respect, of being seen.

When I was a child, very few educators made me feel truly seen. I made decent grades and was a rule-following people pleaser, so I got report card comments that praised what a blessing I was to have in classrooms. And at the same time, I had crippling anxiety and started black-out binge drinking in tenth grade. Still, I was seen as a "pleasure to have in class."

I needed someone to notice, which is why I spent my early years screaming on the inside, "Please notice me!" Yet, when someone would acknowledge my existence, my nervous system would scream louder, "What is happening? Make it stop!" I overrode that second voice for years with alcohol, allowing the "Please notice me!" to take over, followed by some fine print:

"But only the best parts of me that I'm willing to show you. Don't look at the bad stuff or you might not love me."

Until I really started to do the work of being true to myself, which had to start with self-awareness, I was not able to fully live in community. But I needed community in order to start this process. I was living in the barbed protective walls of self-centeredness and control. Within these walls, I was less likely to get hurt but also less likely to truly experience love.

How do we widen our concentric circles and how do we find the path to collective recovery? It starts by recognizing that we do have these circles. That widening these circles means honoring family, connection, belonging, and humanity. Before I understood what it was to be a part of my beloved family, I had to love more. And I knew, somewhere deep within, this included loving myself. But loving myself meant I had to stop lying to myself, and others. And boy, did I tell some doozies throughout my addiction.

I spent years sacrificing authenticity for acceptance. I felt that if people knew who I really was inside, they wouldn't like me, or worse, confirm my worst fears that I'm utterly unlovable. And if I'm unlovable, what does that mean? Would I be kicked out of the club, the family, the village? We need community to survive and feel safe. Our lives depend on it. However, we don't have to pretend, nor lead with our false selves, which will only derail our connection to community. We can learn about our true selves, and then take what we've learned into the world.

STEP FOUR PRACTICE:
Your Action Plan

Get out your markers or paints and open to a blank page in your journal, a large piece of paper, or a poster board. On a second page, write the heading "Action Plan." This is going to be a unique art project. While you create, you are going to make an action plan to honor humanity. You may want to split this up in different chunks, or you can knock it out in one sitting. Whatever feels doable for you.

1. Draw a circle and imagine yourself at the center, use your favorite color or maybe your favorite thing. (My color of choice is magenta and, of course, a butterfly.) Fill your circle with doodles of what makes you happy. While you're doodling, connect with your deepest self and ask if there is anything you need or if you have any unresolved feelings. Jot down an action to meet that need or heal that feeling on your action list.

2. Draw a larger circle, doodling all the things you love about your family and/or community. Smile as you think of them. As you doodle, think of a random act of kindness you could do. Jot it on your action list.

3. Draw an even bigger circle that includes all of humanity. Smile as you think of this largest family, including those you do not like or fear. Include those you find easy to love. Doodle all that you love or all that you are passionate about.

You could bring in collage elements as well, with pictures or words that embody what honoring humanity means to you. Now, think of something that might benefit all within your largest circle(s). Could you donate blood or sign up to be a bone marrow donor? Might you be able to donate to a cause that is doing the work of honoring your largest family? Add that to your action plan.

Place your art in a spot where you will see it regularly, and maybe others will see it, too, so you have the opportunity to connect with others and share the idea of your shared humanity. Take your action list and add it to your calendar or planner. (I am a planner person. I love to-do lists and planning—but the actual action is the important part.) Most importantly, begin living your plan in the world, honoring the most beloved family of all, the world around us.

PART TWO

Be True to Yourself

This above all—to thine own self be true,

And it must follow, as the night the day,

Thou canst not then be false to any man.

—Polonius, *Hamlet*, Act I, Scene 3

CHAPTER FIVE

What Is Truth?

Daddy has a metaphor for spiritual seekers. He says that some folks can just skim across life like water bugs. They stay at surface level, busy with the day-to-day business of existing, just content with being water bugs. Then, there are those of us who are meant to be deep divers. We can try to fit in with the water bugs, but it's likely we'll feel quite lost up there. So, we dive deep to find what's hiding under the surface, exploring the depths for meaning. Most of the deep divers I know have been through something transformational, whether it's addiction, loss, mental health struggles, etc. We have discovered that we have to dive deep in order to survive.

Sitting at my writing table/kitchen table, amid the to-do lists and crumbs, I picked up the phone and asked Daddy what he thought about the words: "Be true to yourself."

He replied, that old Daddy smile apparent in his voice, "It's to be clear about who you really are and how you really are, not how people may see you, but who you are at your core. It means that you are a child of God . . . but so is everyone else. There is humility there too. You're not too pumped up or too small. Self-honesty is at the heart of it."

We went on to talk about pizza night, puppies, and our weekly plans, but as a good papa and priest, he circled back to the message at hand: "Being clear with who you are and then being true to that can be really hard for all of us, especially for those who have not dealt with their demons. Many of us can't be true to ourselves and be a water bug at the same time. You have to know who you are in order to dive down deep."

To dig down deep, we need to learn about the deep collective wisdom beneath the constant internal monologue that plays on repeat in our minds, even when we don't notice it. And to get down there, we need to get a shovel, a backhoe, and sometimes, a freaking excavator.

Because whether it's journaling, meditation, or mindful movement, contemplation grants us the space to observe and open ourselves to that deep wisdom, and to our deepest compassion. I am most judgmental of others when my access to the portal of collective wisdom is not accessible. If I'm stuck in a space where I'm unable to turn inward for contemplation (whether due to outward circumstances or forgetting who I am for a day or two), I tend to operate from a shallower perspective, which always gets me into trouble. Being true to yourself requires self-awareness, and I had no self-awareness until I started a practice of contemplation. A complete contemplation practice involves meditation, prayer, and self-examination—any of these three can be helpful, but taken together, they are magic. And there is no fine print to follow.

Contemplation is a wholly personal act. What works for me may not work for you, but as we commit to self-awareness practices we find that being true to ourselves is more than a goal or quick fix but a deep and powerful practice that requires repetition and commitment. I've been a reluctant long-distance runner for years. In the space between the huffs and puffs on the trail, I discovered that being true to myself is a lot like running. We learn that truth by "lacing up," finding a steady pace in our practice, maybe trying new routes along the way, and adjusting our plan for what works and what doesn't. Sometimes we eat dirt and get hurt along the way. But if we keep practicing, we keep getting stronger, more agile, and more able to understand ourselves and those around us.

WE CONNECT THROUGH
OUR DARKEST TRUTHS

I was in kindergarten. My friends and I were passing a crayon box under the table and giggling about it. (This is what I remember, y'all. Who knows what was really going on, but whatever it was, I cannot think of a scenario that warranted what came to pass.) My entire table was called into the hallway and paddled for the infraction of . . . whatever rule it was that we broke. I was last to get off the school bus that day. I didn't want to go home.

If my parents knew I got paddled, I'd be in so much trouble.

"How was your day, Maggie?"

"Fine. Good."

I don't know what lesson my teacher intended to teach me that morning by spanking me in front of my friends, but the lesson my five-year-old mind got was: lying works. I told Mama this story when I was thirty-five years old. She cried. I learned that she would not have disowned me forever if she found out I had been paddled. Instead, she would've marched right into the school that day, beaten down the door of the teacher and the principal, and demanded to know why five-year-olds were being beaten over crayons (or anything, for that matter). She would've started a mission to end corporal punishment in schools in southern Georgia.

But I didn't know. So, I lied. For thirty years, I lied.

It's not like I went around lying on purpose. I wasn't a pathological liar. It was more like the lies of denial, dis-ease, and convenience. There were the lies where I ignored my internal sensor (the "this doesn't feel right" bellyache) and chose what would win me affection, attention, and a spot in the crowd. Then there were also the lies that would smooth things over and avoid a fight. There were lies that made me feel like I was less of a bother or burden. And there were the lies to myself that would make me happy in the moment but hurt in the long run. *The bills can wait. You study better when you're drunk. You are a good buzzed driver. You were drunk so you deserved it. Do the cocaine, you're drunk already, it's fine, it's fine. You're fine. It's fine. YOLO.*

When you can't tell the true from the false anymore, it's just one big vortex of lies. That was me, swirling around in all the doozies I told myself and others until I couldn't tell which way was up. Pretty soon, I had nowhere to turn, except for one clear solution in my mind that would solve the entire mess I had created (besides continuing to drink to oblivion). The lies that come from depression and alcoholism are really good at sounding like the truth. The lies that told me that I was better off dead would be where I found my rock bottom. And the beginning of my truth.

Gloria Steinem has a famous quote: "The truth will set you free but first it will piss you off." For me, the truth was scary as shit. Like, who the hell am I? I had my first drink at twelve years old and had been lying and people-pleasing since before five. Who was I without that? And if you knew the truth of who I really was, would you even love me? Who would be pissed off by my truth?

> Often, we don't know our truth until we see it in someone else.

When someone shares something about themselves that resonates deeply within us, we see it. "Oh, my goodness, me too!" or "I feel seen." Hearing another's darkest truths—especially if they've found their way—can open us up to seeing our own truths with the hope that we can find our way too.

ONE IS TOO MANY AND A THOUSAND IS NEVER ENOUGH

As I sat in my pajamas and stiff new bathrobe with my hospital ID bracelet, the residential counselor knocked on the open door to my room to tell me it was time for a chat. The place smelled like ammonia and hot dogs. If it weren't for all of the young patients, I'd swear I was in a nursing home. I'd been there for a day and only just agreed to come out of my room. I was in the detox and mental health wing of a hospital in South Florida after an unsuccessful suicide attempt. I resented being there with addicts. I was convinced that my problem was that I wanted to die and couldn't find the energy to deal with all the problems that had built up around me. Forever sleep seemed like the only answer.

His name was Bob. He was bald with tattoos and a few gold teeth. My head was down, as I messed with my bathrobe and fingernails, anything to keep me from looking at this man. He asked me a few icebreaker questions.

"How much do you drink?"

You don't beat around the bush, do you, Bob?

"A little, but that's not why I'm here."

"Humor me. How much, say, in a weekend?" He had a Brooklyn accent and smelled of cigarettes, which made me jones for my next smoke. Looking at the clock, we had thirty minutes until they unlocked the patio so we could smoke (every three hours, quarter to the hour).

"Maybe two a night, twice a week?" That was the answer I gave . . . my "I am a normal drinker" answer.

"Hmmm, that's interesting. Because I saw your labs. Do you have a history of liver disease? Because on paper I see more than two drinks twice a week."

"Oh . . ."

"Humor me again. Can I tell you a little bit about myself?"

He proceeded to tell me about his addiction to more: more booze, more money, more shopping, more sex, more sweets, more scratch-off tickets, more attention, more, more, more.

"One is too many and a thousand is never enough," he said.

This man, opposite me in every way on the outside, told me my story.

This happens over and over, in twelve-step rooms, corners of social media, and safe spaces where people show up whole-heartedly. In those little nooks of humanity, we find out we aren't alone. Bob didn't have to tell me his story that day in the hospital. He was going to be there either way. But he took a moment to share and then listen and then share some more.

And he gave me the story of hope that I didn't have yet. He had been to the depths that I was experiencing, and he'd lived to tell about it. He sat there in his own truth, offering stories of self-acceptance, showing me what could be my truth too.

There is this uncomfortable space when we start to truly see ourselves. It's a space where we know that we want to change, but we don't have the time under our belt nor the tools to get there. This space between who we want to become and who we are now can be painful. It's hard not to sit in self-loathing. It's hard to look at all of ourselves . . . and accept every single part.

When I was several years sober, my sponsor, Susan, gave me a book called *There Is Nothing Wrong with You* by Cheri Huber. My first thought was, *This book is dumb because there is so much wrong with me.* But I was crying with identification by the end of the first paragraph. From our first days on this planet, we're encouraged to stop having needs. We're taught how to make our baby stop crying (babies cry because that's their only way of communicat-ing their needs), instead of thinking, *My baby is crying to tell me they are a whole human with needs and wants and for me to listen and not just try to get them to shut up.*

For many years, I was a self-help information collector. I loved reading books that promised to fix me or outlined my problems. The information may have been helpful for some, but I used it as proof that there was something wrong with me, proof that I didn't belong, proof that I was hopeless.

> When I opened up to the idea that there was nothing wrong with me, it empowered me in a whole new kind of way. It offered me a chance to look at my life through the lens of truth.

This was my first experience of self-acceptance, self-love, and true honesty. There was nothing wrong with that little girl in kindergarten who got paddled. There was nothing wrong with that woman standing in front of a man she wasn't sure if she was supposed to marry, or the woman standing in front of the military recruiter saying "yes" when she wanted to say "no." There was nothing wrong with the woman who got too drunk way too often. There is nothing wrong with the woman who is writing this with a brain tumor and three kids on screens so that I can have a moment to write.

It took facing all the truths over all the years, sitting in the pain, and forgiving myself (over and over) to start this journey of self-discovery.

RECOVERING THE TRUTH

I did it. Thirty days and thirty nights of hard, boring sobriety, the longest month of my life. The chair I'm sitting on is cold, the room is cold, and because it's South Florida and always above 90 degrees Fahrenheit, I hadn't thought to bring a sweater. I fidget the entire meeting, wondering if everyone can tell. Do I look thirty days sober? I can't wait until it's my turn! I wonder what it will feel like holding the coin in my hand. Oh, it's time. The moment I've been waiting for.

"At this meeting, we have a chip system to denote lengths of sobriety. If you've heard something tonight and want to give this way of life a try, come on up and pick up a white chip."

A few folks stroll up and get their white chips . . . *I'm up next!*

"And if you've got thirty consecutive days and nights of sobriety, come on up and get a chip."

This is my moment! I go up and grab it. A short round of applause and I'm back in my chair, face beet red. And the caller is moving on to the next chip. That was it. Now what? Ugh. I have to start counting again to the next one. Thirty more days. Oh God. I rub the coin in my hand, feeling stupid for getting so excited when I notice it doesn't just say, "Thirty days."

It reads: "To thine own self be true."

There in that cold chair, I'm fifteen again, in my floral dress and Doc Martens, impatiently enduring my dad reciting the 3 Things. It hits me like a lightning bolt. Recovery is how I'm going to learn to be true to myself. Staring at the inscription on that little plastic poker chip, I decided to embark on the adventure of recovering my truth.

I couldn't keep up the "Tale of Two Maggies" any longer. I was defined by all the outside stuff—the career, the marriage, my possessions. I was led by circumstances, not by virtue. I looked outside myself for what was true. I no longer had an internal navigation system to show me the way. Alcohol, self-doubt, and external validation took the place of any internal truth.

There was no more running from all the lies that had built up over the course of my drinking. I'd told most of them for self-preservation, merely to uphold the Good Maggie pillar of the tale. I came into the searing bright light to realize that after all the lies, the people-pleasing, and the drinking, I had no idea who I was.

Collective recovery is about finding our internal GPS again. It's about diving deep and discovering our true north, about discerning the true from the false, and discarding the old ideas that aren't working for us anymore. It's unlearning the conditioning that drives us to operate against our own best interest, and emerging into the truth that collective recovery offers us all.

THE PATH OF TRUTH

I got sick in July 2020, and by September, I could hardly get out of bed. After eight weeks of feeling miserable, I wasn't sure I'd ever improve, which led me to despair.

By the first week of September, I was no longer able to work out or do jiujitsu. I couldn't run or lift weights. I could barely walk to the bathroom or the kitchen. Standing to cook was out of the question, as were chores and parenting. I didn't think I was going to make it through this. One morning I prayed the prayer of desperation. Mostly it was just "Help," but more specifically it was, "Please remind me what there is to live for. Either make me better or make me worse, I can't live like this anymore."

The answer to my prayer came in the form of Julia Cameron's book, *The Artist's Way for Parents*. I had tried to read it a couple of years prior when I was trying to be less of a yelling mommy. It didn't catch. This time, it latched on to my soul. It was as if my prayer of desperation invited the universe to open me up so I could receive new ideas and much-needed answers. I started and finished the book in twenty-four hours. It motivated me to get out the watercolor set I'd purchased at the beginning of the pandemic, somewhere between the succulent hoarding stage and the making my own pizza dough era.

I played with the paints tentatively at first. Then the kids wanted to take part, so we spent entire afternoons painting. Not only did I have a new pep in my step, but I also remembered that I had Julia Cameron's older book, *The Artist's Way*, sitting on my shelf collecting dust. I took out her book and started her twelve-week course in earnest. I was painting more, which was great, but I also realized that I had been hiding my desire to write. And so, my creative recovery began, even though I was in the biggest health struggle of my life.

The first week I started the morning pages, Julia Cameron's daily practice in which you stream-of-consciousness write at least three pages first thing in the morning, my world opened up. To honor my eight-year-old creative self, I added watercolors to the pages. Solutions I'd been trying to work out suddenly appeared on the page. Encouraged by this, I started asking questions I'd never thought to ask before. I did the weekly assignments in earnest and grew by the day. The healing was happening in my psyche, as well as in my physical form. I fully believe that book saved my life, and it inspired me to write this one.

When we embark on this journey of self-acceptance, we discover the truth of who we really are, not who we think our parents want us to be, or the person we have always thought we were going to be. We find out who we are deep inside.

> The truth is much more subtle than the hustle of ambition, the pressure of expectations, or any of the things we pile on ourselves from the outside.

The labels and the failures and the keeping up with Joneses and the Kardashians, the social media highlight reel, and the latest rumors coming out of the PTO meetings . . . these are not your truths. Your North Star sparkles much more brightly.

In order to find our truth, we have to dive deep, as Daddy said. We have to meet ourselves; many of us will be doing this for the first time. How do we do this? Stillness. We have to get quiet and still. When we do, we'll begin to see what is going on in our minds and bodies. It will be frustrating at first, because it will feel like we're doing it wrong. The only way to do it wrong is by not trying. When we meet ourselves with stillness and we meet whatever comes up with compassion, we see that it's okay. There is nothing wrong with us. We find the strength and curiosity to keep going. As we progress, we are gifted with glimpses of intuition, those "I don't know how I know, I just know" moments. These gifts keep coming, the more we honor this practice of stillness.

When Daddy first gave his sermon to the St. Andrews graduating class of 1994 and he said, "Be true to yourself," he was asking those seniors to follow their true north, to make decisions that were in line with their inner values. The essence of that is to stop lying to yourself and to follow the real you, the "steadfast, loyal, honest, and just" you.

When we get honest with ourselves, we learn what is *for* us and what is *not* for us. We start yearning for the deep dive, just to find out what's down there. Deep divers like us get tired of living on the surface like water bugs. Because to find that glimmer of the spirit, we must be willing to swim down and find it.

STEP FIVE PRACTICE:
The Morning Dump

One of my spiritual teachers, Durga Leela of Yoga of Recovery, taught me RPM (rise, pee, meditate). For me that morphed into rise, pee, morning pages, or as I like to call them, the morning dump.

Morning pages, prescribed by Julia Cameron in *The Artist's Way*, are three pages of stream-of-consciousness writing, longhand with pen and paper. But sometimes I don't have three pages of time. And then, if I don't have the time, I avoid writing the three pages altogether.

So, here's what I want you to do. I want you to take a morning dump. Okay, I know it's crass, but we all talk about poop way more than we admit anyway (especially if you're a parent)! And as a caretaker of both children and my aging parents, it's a major topic in our lives.

Think of it this way. Whether you're actually doing your writing while on or off the pot, take the same amount of time for writing as it takes you to do your morning business. If the day before you ate a lot of bad stuff, you might need to take longer. If you've been drinking a lot of water, and been treating yourself right, you might have less to say. But take the same amount of time you reserve for la toilette and use it to write your morning dump.

Here's what you do:

1. Commit to seven days. Put it on your to-do list and wake up ten to thirty-ish minutes earlier for the next week.

2. Find your yummiest pen and paper combo and set them in a spot that you will not be able to say that you forgot—by the coffee. on the kitchen table, by your pillow, on top of your phone . . . or the toilet—whatever will help.

3. Then, rise . . . pee . . . write down your morning dump.

The reason this is so great is that it helps us skim off all the unnecessary noise in our brains; it helps us identify our self-talk and unresolved emotions and it helps us get down to our deepest intuition . . . sometimes. That's why I suggest doing it for a week.

And then, keep going until the magic happens.

PS: If you prefer afternoon dumps or you have more time in the evening. do it then. Just don't skip it. You don't want to get backed up!

CHAPTER SIX

Finding Home through Self-Discovery

I have a confession to make. I have the warring mindsets of wanting my child to be free and wanting to keep them safe from judgment, insults, and harm.

Clayton, our middle child, has been a unique soul since they came to the earth. The animated movie *Frozen* came out when Clayton was two; in addition to watching on repeat, they fell in love with a hat that had a flowing "Elsa" ponytail attached.

"That hat is for girls!" an unsupervised little girl of eight or nine yelled at him in the toy aisle, and then to us, "Why is he wearing a girl's hat?"

There was some expectation management on the part of my Marine Corps husband and unlearning of our own ideas on what little boys are "supposed to" play with as Clayton played dress-up and dolls, makeup and glitter, and all things unicorn, rainbow, and sparkly; they still do. Clayton has taught us that clothing and toys do not have a gender, and that gender identity and expression exist on a spectrum.

Now, we live in rural southern Georgia, not exactly a region known for its understanding and acceptance of gender fluidity. We're not too far from the state line over which gay and trans kids are targeted by legislation, and where parents like me are referred to as "groomers." When Clayton wants to go to school wearing mascara or dons a dress to the all-you-can-eat buffet, my first reaction is to clench up and want to (and sometimes do) make them go change.

Clayton regularly makes statements like: "Mom, I'm nonbinary, and my pronouns are he/him, they/them."

That particular proclamation happened in the drive-through at McDonald's one afternoon. Clayton said it in the most casual, yet matter-of-fact way, I had to pick my jaw up off my lap. It wasn't that I was surprised by the conversation, I was surprised by the confidence. With all my efforts at protecting this child, and superficially and sadly my own reputation as a parent, Clayton is 100 percent true to who they are. While they have the anxiety they inherited from both sides, their self-confidence doesn't waver.

I was never so sure of who I was at age two or nine or twelve or even this morning.

THE HEALING POWERS OF SELF-DISCOVERY

Rewind to Maggie at the age of eight or nine. There is a family photo of us on the move from one state to another. I'm hard to miss in the photo, sporting my cropped haircut (which I begged for) and clutching my sketchbook.

Oh, the haircut. I had beautiful blond curls as a toddler, much to Grandpapa's delight (I was bald for an oddly long time). He would tell stories at the dinner table in my teens about how he wasn't sure if I'd ever get hair. I did eventually. And it was pretty and blond and curly . . . until Mary Lou Retton and my bestie Molly came along. Molly had a short haircut and Mary Lou was a gold-medal gymnast showing off her shaggy bowl cut on cereal boxes. Like so many kids my age, I wanted to be her!

I begged Mama. I begged and begged and begged. Over time, I wore her down. But my victory was clipped by the sad look on the hairstylist's face—and my mom's—at the idea that I might look like a boy. For about 3.7 seconds, I got a little worried too. Then I realized how good I felt, light and free of my thick hair. I looked exactly like Mary Lou Retton!

As time passed and girls were getting perms and growing their hair out, I forgot how much I loved my short hair. It was the 1980s and girls were supposed to have long hair (and big bangs and perms and highlights. etc.). So, I tried to grow my hair. But then, in my mid-twenties, the pixie cut came back in style among those bold enough to try it. I felt so hot with a pixie cut (and way cooler in the South's heat). Women stopped me daily to tell me how brave I was.

"I could never do that," they would say. "But it looks great on you."

Over the years, I'd try to grow it out—sometimes thinking it would make me feel more feminine, or that it would be the "fix" I was looking for when I'd forgotten the truth that there's nothing wrong with me. I never made it through the awkward grow-out stage before chopping it all off. And then, I'd feel like I'd found myself again.

So, there I was in our family picture, with my short hair, hugging a sketchbook. During that year, I was constantly drawing. I clung to my long, skinny Crayola markers and my blank sketchpad, its pages full of possibility. I used to draw a picture of a church in a field of wildflowers. I drew it over and over. I wrote poems and practiced cursive. I drew faces and practiced eyes and trees and birds and clouds. And then one day, I stopped. I can tell you the exact moment I stopped. It involved cake.

At school, we had something called Friday School, a program devoted to the arts. Some sessions we did pottery and painting, but one session was dedicated to cake decorating. For our final project, we were to bake and decorate our own cake by ourselves. I selected an Easter egg cake mold and decorated with pink, blue, and yellow piping on white icing. It was an impressive masterpiece from an eight-year-old; I was proud. So proud that I demanded to carry it.

"Can't I help you with that, sweetie?" My dad tried to pry the thing out of my hands, but I assured him, "I've got it."

I did not have it. I dropped that masterpiece right there on the curb in front of my school. The intricate icing that adorned my beautiful egg was now a brown blob, and I was an inconsolable mess. The teacher tried to fix it, but it felt like she was stabbing me in the heart with every swipe of her plastic knife. I wanted to melt. I wanted to disappear. The lesson I took away from that day was that the risk was too great. Creating was too painful.

As an adult on my recovery path, I bought myself an Easter egg cake pan and a cake decorating kit. It wasn't Easter (October actually), but I made the prettiest darn Halloween egg you ever did see, and eight-year-old Maggie was delighted. The whole family ate that cake and got messy with it. My husband and the kids got to witness me honoring my eight-year-old self with this ritual of creativity. This is what being true to myself means to me. Honoring the thing in me that lights me up, that makes me *me*, even when it's painful and messy.

Clayton draws like I did before the cake incident. They draw and they dress how they want despite my warnings that people outside our home may bully or question their choices. Clayton tried out for a solo in chorus—after little more than a pep talk from me—and the night of the performance, they flawlessly belted out "Believer" by Imagine Dragons.

Watching this child, who is so like me in a lot of ways, work through their anxiety and fear of failure, seeing their drive to keep creating day after day, is teaching me how to be true to myself.

We're breaking generational curses together, one miracle at a time.

THE FREEDOM OF SELF-DISCOVERY

After my egg cake accident, I hid my passion away in a safe place where it would never be devastated again. I loved dance, but that was because I wanted to be like the other girls who went out for dance. When I married my first husband, I became a huge basketball fan. We spent a great deal of our time together watching basketball. I knew players' names and had a favorite team (pretty sure my favorite team was his favorite team). After we divorced and I quit drinking, I realized I'm not really a basketball fan. I liked supporting his hobby and being with him, but after we divorced, I realized that I just really liked to drink. Now I appreciate that my eighteen-year-old son likes the sport, that my dad watches March Madness, but I no longer have to pretend I like it.

I'm reminded of the scene from the movie *Runaway Bride* where Julia Roberts's character Maggie (coincidence? I think not) realizes she doesn't know what kind of eggs she likes because she always likes whatever her fiancé favors . . . and there's a scene where she's in her kitchen trying all the different eggs. I had to do the same thing, experimenting to find out who I was.

To have a (mostly) daily look at myself, I still do those morning pages, aka morning dump. I write for thirty minutes—sometimes less, sometimes more. I aim for three pages of stream-of-consciousness writing each day. I keep showing up on the page until the magic happens. I don't have to love it; I just have to do it. My ego is one hell of a censor and will tell me the entire time that this is dumb. I just keep writing and asking my HP (Higher Power) what I need to write about. I write the little annoyances and the big grievances, what I see out the window. I write letters to my eight-year-old self, my teenage self, my yesterday self. I do an inventory or a to-do list. Whatever comes out of my hand. And in the process, I come to know myself more and more each day, connecting to what I love, what I care about, what I prioritize, and what I need in life to be happy and fulfilled, to be true to myself.

Throughout the practice of the morning dump, I also learned that I don't give myself permission to be messy unless I really write and process what I'm going through. There's so much tension between who I am now and who I think I should be (especially when I haven't done my morning writing in a while), and I don't see that unless I'm writing. The process of writing about that tension, acknowledging that it's there, and then giving myself permission to be just as I am—a sometimes messy but always worthy human—heals me every time.

There is so much joy in the process of self-discovery.

I used to operate from two personas, Good Maggie or Bad Maggie. Good Maggie said her prayers, went to church, and laughed at jokes, even when they weren't funny. Bad Maggie got into all kinds of trouble. Through my process of self-discovery, I've been able to accept all the parts of myself. Good Maggie and Bad Maggie are no longer separate. I have lived long enough and learned enough about myself to integrate into one human form known as Maggie. When I was first figuring this whole thing out though, I fought to compartmentalize each aspect of myself. I had sober life, work life, fitness life, military spouse life, mom life, and within each, I had a distinct personality and set of friends. My lives rarely overlapped. I kept everything separate— much like with the Good Maggie and Bad Maggie—but much harder to keep track of and much more subtle.

I wasn't lying on purpose, however, one group didn't know about my sobriety, and another group didn't know I was vegan, and this other group thought I was so organized, while another cherished my "hot mess mom" persona.

On the weekends, I would completely ignore or neglect to call my sponsor, even if I needed her guidance and the comfort of my twelve-step friends, because I was lost in my "Family Maggie" self. It was social media that blurred the lines of my carefully cordoned-off worlds. From the safety of the keyboard, I could be more vulnerable and honest. All the friends from the lives of all the Maggies were there in one place. I had real-life moments where my worlds collided and boy, were they uncomfortable. When a work friend brought up a sobriety quote I posted, or a military spouse congratulated me on a fitness challenge, or a sober friend asked how that work thing was going, I felt the disorienting blur of my worlds melting together.

Like all of us, I'm still learning how to integrate all of these parts, and it can be weird at times. My husband's work friend once saw my brain tumor story on social media and mentioned it to him. I got queasy thinking she might be judging me for being so real in public . . . or for my parenting or political posts. I even caught myself asking, "Well, what did she say?" My people-pleaser part wanted desperately to read into her words to find out whether or not she liked me.

And then I remembered who I am, a messy recovering person who is free to be exactly as I am. I had been longing for this, for belonging. When I let go and just lived, I was finally free.

The Discovery Inventory

Recovery was my portal to self-discovery. It didn't happen overnight. It has been many a yearlong process. And it started and continues with what we call in twelve-step recovery "a fearless and searching moral inventory." Bill W., one of the founders of Alcoholics Anonymous, explains the inventory in what we lovingly call the *Big Book of Alcoholics Anonymous*. He compares it to an inventory that a business would do. To have a successful business, you have to know what's on your shelves, all salable and unsalable goods right? Well, the same goes for a moral inventory. We take an honest look at our resentments, fears, and wrongs done.

1. Get a blank piece of paper and hold it so it is landscape. Fold it into three sections. You may need multiple sheets. Also have your journal handy for any "aha" moments that come.

2. In the first column you made with your creases, list all the things that piss you off—all the people, places, and things.

3. When you run out of steam with your list, go to the second column. Write a short description next to each item in the first column: Why are you angry at this person? How did that place hurt you? What did this thing do to you?

4. Go to column 3. In this column, you're going to get down to causes and conditions. Ask yourself why this is disturbing you. When you get an answer, ask why again and again, until you get down to the core of the matter. You will probably find that it is affecting your sense of family, self, or faith. Maybe it's because you're afraid you're going to lose something you love, or you'll not get something you want. Take a moment to journal on what you can do about any of the items.

Final step: Forgive yourself for doing the best you could with the resources that you had at the time. If you can, forgive those on your list for doing the best they could with the resources they had at the time. If it's not possible, and if the harm done was simply too great, that's okay too. But it all starts by just saying or writing the words "I forgive you" even if you don't feel it yet. As you move through the following chapters and exercises (and life in general), you will find that forgiveness is like a flowering vine: it spreads out over time, never erasing what has happened, but offering something more beautiful in its place.

CHAPTER SEVEN

Embracing the Truths of Self-Acceptance

G et up, Get up, Get up!"

Our recruit drill commanders (or RDCs, as we call them) screamed at us as they banged on trash cans, jarring us out of our sleep. It was time for battle stations—our final test in order to pass boot camp and go into the fleet as sailors. We all scrambled out of our racks, donning our battle dress, canteens, and helmets. I stood on the line with my shipmates, ready for whatever was in store, shaking in my literal boots. One thing that hadn't been covered in the training leading up to this test: what happens if you have to pee when you get ripped out of bed for a war scenario? No one else was running to the head (that's the Navy term for bathroom).

Do I just hold it? I guess I just hold it.

Have you ever had to run with a very full bladder? Can you guess what happened next? I could either walk or I could pee my dungarees. So, I walked.

"ARE YOU ALREADY QUITTING, RECRUIT?!" an RDC barked behind me.

I picked up the pace and proceeded to pee down my legs. Panic set in, I started crying and stopped running. I stood there, enduring the barking in my face for a few moments before turning to walk back to our barracks. I hid the evidence as best I could and waited for my shipmates to return victorious. I'd never felt like such a fuckup as I did in those moments and the days that followed. Thankfully, I got another chance with another division the following week. I went to the bathroom in the middle of the night and laid in wait, ready for the banging to begin.

I jumped out of my rack ready to go and I rocked battle stations. But what I didn't rock was accepting the humanness of my first go-round. I failed. I learned. I did it again, but until I learned to really heal and accept my whole story, I replayed every scenario of how it could have gone different over and over again on a loop in my head.

Why couldn't I have just been super hard-core and ran with pee-pee pants? Our first station was the pool so it wouldn't have mattered anyway—what would I have been able to prove? The internal dialogue would go into overdrive, replaying the experience and reliving each moment of shame and stress. It would take me years to even notice that I was carrying all of this. The work of recovery—and the practice of daily writing—helped me see and confront the unnecessary and untrue ways of thinking about myself and others.

Self-acceptance has been the juiciest, most beautiful side effect of the "true to yourself" path, and I believe it resulted from the practice of contemplation. This practice has led me to acknowledging and recovering from paralyzing perfectionism and has given me permission to be a full messy human in times of success and in the times when I'm fucking it all up.

ACCEPTING OUR HARDEST DAYS

My hands were shaking as I put on my uniform web belt. We weren't allowed to have our belts or shoes on the inpatient psych floor of the naval hospital, but I had a special visitor. I was dressed as nicely as I could be in my uniform, minus my rank insignia pins (no sharp objects allowed), but my James wouldn't care; he just wanted to see his mama. We sat there on the cold, hard food court bench, both of us trying to figure out how to be together in such a weird and exposed meeting place.

"Mommy, why can't I see you at your house?" James asked. *Oh, my heart.*

"Baby, you know how when you are sick you have to go to the doctor? And when people are really sick sometimes they have to stay with the doctor at the hospital?" He nodded as I stared into his gorgeous four-year-old brown cow eyes, wishing we were anywhere but here. "Well, mommy's brain is really sick right now and I have to stay here to get better."

After he caught me up on his preschool adventures and had all the food court items he could stand, his dad, my ex-husband, pulled me aside. "This is too much for him. I hate seeing you here and I know he hates seeing you here. Please consider that this isn't only about you."

"Are you saying you don't want him to visit me?" I was trying so hard to keep my tears in so James couldn't see.

"I don't know what I'm saying, Maggie. Just focus on getting better. For him."

And with that I watched them walk away, James running and skipping up the ramped hallway. My consolation was that he was happy and healthy, and his father gave him a stable and loving home. One that I couldn't give him.

A month later, I got the call that they were moving out of state. James's dad got a job he couldn't refuse and since I was in no shape to care for my son, he was going too. We had promised one another in our divorce that we wouldn't have a messy fight for custody of our child and that we would always do what was best for him. I just never imagined that leaving me was what was best for him. I ached for my baby daily, and when I shamed myself for being a horrible mother, I was left with the truth that if I fought for that child to live with me, it would be for me, and not for him.

But I tell you what, the pain of losing custody of a child is something you can't know until you've been there.

I was divorced, $45,000 in consumer debt, facing the end of my military career, and my baby was going to his first day of kindergarten without his mommy. I was sober, thanks to my first inpatient visit, but I wasn't well. I was in and out of inpatient care and wanted to die almost the entire first year. It wasn't until I received a course of twelve electroconvulsive treatments (shock therapy) that I thought I might survive any of this.

Would I always be such a fuckup?

I'd love to share that I found a magic pill or easy button and my life got better overnight, that I committed right away to self-acceptance and never looked back. The truth is that the journey was an uphill battle of veritable Whack-a-Mole. One crisis or character defect at a time would pop up and demand attention, resolution, or amends.

> And one at a time, I stood in the fucked-up-ness of it all and did the next right thing.

The shame and pain of losing custody of my son would constantly pop up to tell me I was a horrible mother—that good mothers are there for the first days of school and orthodontics visits.

In the beginning, it would knock the wind out of me. But as time passed and I saw what a beautiful human being he was growing into, I was able to accept the unacceptable. Even today, I still get little pangs of grief over what never was, but the self-loathing and shame are now only a memory that I get to share with those facing the unacceptable.

You've heard it said that we can't truly love others until we love ourselves. And that is true. Sort of. There's a reason why being part of a family comes first in this book. My twelve-step family, my husband, and my biological family, too, loved me through the hardest times of my life, when I could not love myself. I needed to depend on them, and I needed them to need me, so that I could find the strength to stand on my own and have the courage to be true to myself.

When I met my husband, I was full of self-loathing and in the grips of addiction. I know I loved him almost immediately, but it would be years of self-discovery and learning to take care of myself, to love myself, and accept myself as I am.

Love isn't a one-way street. My now-husband has showered me with kindness since day one and has seen me at my best and worst (he was the one who gave me rides to shock treatments back in the day, after all), but before I truly experienced self-acceptance, there was a feeling of unworthiness about receiving his loving gestures. His love and my own self-love have helped me smooth that unworthy spot, but even now, he still has to challenge my self-deprecating remarks at times.

If you're like me and you've hit rock bottom, you know what it is to regrow and redevelop. Only then can we learn to love ourselves and others, to be of service in a way that is authentic and does not compromise our values. Only then can we bake the egg-shaped cakes of our past. You know what they say, you have to frost your own cake before you can frost others (I am the *they* in this scenario). We face the past, or the hard thing in front of us, with self-care and compassion, we sit with that hard thing and the feelings and beliefs that come up.

And then, we model our recovery to those around us, ourselves, and others for giving and receiving love.

PERFECTLY IMPERFECT

Aside from that year of suicidal depression, perfectionism is probably the most painful thing I've had to deal with. I didn't want to do anything unless I already knew how to do it. I'm not sure how I thought everyone else did things. I first got the idea for this book when I was seventeen years old. I kept telling my dad he should write *The 3 Things* book.

It felt urgent to me that he do this, but it wasn't urgent to him. He was fine preaching the 3 Things every now and then when the timing was right. I was restless about it, hoping no one would steal his book idea before he got around to writing it. As time passed, I thought, maybe it wasn't urgent to him because it was my book to write.

I started a Word document in 2010, at age thirty-two. "The 3 Things" are the only words written on that file. I would tell myself, "I'm not a writer." The paralyzing fear of "Who do I think I am?" was my excuse for not writing this book. Perfectionist Maggie—we'll call her Margaret—believes that writers pop out of the womb having entire books lined up for publishing, and as we all know, that's just not the case.

I was named Margaret at birth after my grandmother. Neither of us went by Margaret, I'm a Maggie and she was a Peggy. But every doctor visit, class roster, and official piece of mail had the name Margaret on it—my IDs and social security card. Checks made out to "Maggie" I'd have to endorse as Margaret because that was the name on my bank account. After the brain tumor hospitalization, I was done being Margaret. I prayed to Grandmother for forgiveness (and ran it by my family, out of reverence) and for my forty-fourth birthday, I legally changed my name to Maggie. The weight that lifted when I became Maggie for real was immense. It was a ceremony—discarding the perfectionist, Margaret, that I'd been allowing to run my life.

Once I realized my perfectionism was about pain avoidance, I did my best to let it go. If I don't ever mess anything up, I won't feel the pain of failure or embarrassment or public ridicule, or the devastation of seeing my Easter egg cake in a brown, crumbled heap on the curb. If I don't ever start the thing, then I don't have to live up to the impossible expectation of doing it perfectly. I save myself from the pain of the dropped cake. Playing it safe became my go-to option. But it was quickly followed by the worst fate of them all, the pain of regret.

> To avoid that pain of regret, I had to confront the pain of trying and failing. I had to rediscover my own creativity, my own messiness, the beauty of my own imperfections.

I first learned this concept from Brené Brown's book, *The Gifts of Imperfection*. I've read it multiple times, when I was in a space where I was incredibly hard on myself and felt like everything I did was not enough. There was a nonstop judgmental dialogue in my head questioning everything I did and said, as well as everyone around me. But as I learned through Brené's famed book, self-loathing was actually just the act of not giving myself permission to be a human being, which meant I wasn't letting other people be human beings either. What high expectations I held all of us to! We say in recovery rooms that expectations are resentments waiting to happen.

If I'm giving myself permission to be human, that means I'm giving other people permission to be human too—to be imperfect, to drop the cake, and sometimes, to fuck it all up.

THE LIBERATING EXPERIENCE
OF BEING A FUCKUP

How did I learn to recover from the fucked-upness of it all? From the paralyzing perfectionism by which I lived? By messing it all up. By not living up to expectations, my own and others. By being imperfect and feeling the discomfort when I made mistakes. That is where the contemplation part comes in. Contemplation is defined as deep reflective thought or the act of looking thoughtfully at something for some time. So, we look at the stuff we'd rather not see. We write it out and we challenge the lies that tell us we aren't lovable or that we aren't good enough.

We are all human, and we all have our stories of fuckups that we would rather not tell anyone, like ever. But do you know the most liberating part of it all? Being able to share my story of the naval hospital with a woman who is going through something similar. Been there, done that, proudly wearing the proverbial T-shirt. Because my fuckups become the wisdom that help the person beside me if I open up and share. The disbelief when I tell the sordid details of drunken embarrassments and sober shortcomings—and the relief in their faces when they understand they aren't alone—makes all of those things I'd rather not tell anyone, like, ever, become the promise of a better future for someone else.

Now there is a time and a place, y'all. I'm the queen of oversharing, just ask my colleagues up and down the sixth-grade hall. Sometimes it's not even saying it all out loud, it's acknowledging that we're all going through stuff and have been through stuff. It's about holding space for everyone to be messy humans.

Learning to wrestle with my perfectionism, accept my humanity, and forgive myself changed the game for me. As a result, I'm kinder to myself and everyone around me. We are messy human beings, and frankly, it's way more fun to embrace that truth than try to hide it and pretend we're not.

Ever tried to hold in a fart all day long?

That shit is exhausting. And it fucking *hurts*.

The first time I ever said, "My name is Maggie and I'm an alcoholic," was liberating. If I can own this part of myself, which seemed to be the most fucked up, that means there's a solution! If I'm denying the problem, there is no answer. There would be no way to recover from the thing I was most ashamed of, the pee-pee pants I'd made of my life.

THE TREE OF SELF-ACCEPTANCE

Michele has been my recovery sponsor for about twelve of my sixteen years of sobriety. She tells a story about her metaphorical tree, and it's my favorite story of hers. Here's my version of her tree story:

I'm a tree. The tallest, best kind of Christmas tree. You can't quite tell from the outside that I'm a tree—the shape is there but I'm heavy and weighed down with a bunch of stuff that's not mine, junky stuff that's hanging from my branches. There's an old tire, some Silly String, and I got toilet-papered at some point. There are a few dirty diapers—horrible, nasty, smelly things. A kiddie pool. A mattress. Each piece is a lie I've told or lived in.

As I learn the process of self-examination and as I continue to live my truth, I see that this old tire (a lie I've been telling) isn't mine anymore. This boot without a match (a role I've been trying to play) isn't mine anymore. As I identify each thing that's not mine anymore, I'm free to either discard it or appreciate its presence. I've been in this process for years now, and I smell like a tree, I look like a tree, hell, I even have twinkle lights. The junk that's on my tree today? That junk gives me personality and lessons that are still to be learned.

Sometimes I'll throw an old banana peel up there for good measure so I can say, "Oh that's not my truth, let me clean up this mess I've made." My tree of self-acceptance invites others to take care of their own tree. Now I have an excuse to keep a tree with twinkle lights year-round. It's my tree of self-acceptance!

A common saying in addiction recovery spaces is "We're only as sick as our secrets." What stays in the dark, hidden inside of us, grows and festers and eventually starts to harm us. What we are willing to get honest about, or shine light on, loses its power and its hold on our insides and actions. This requires sitting with the discomfort and the risk of sharing, but it leads to freedom.

I didn't tell a soul the battle stations pee story until long after my retirement. The day I told someone, jokingly admitting what had happened as a protective reflex, I experienced immediate relief. Releasing that truth allowed me space to look

at why I had held it so tight, and finally I was able to forgive—
and accept—myself.

And to answer my earlier question: No, I would not always be
a fuckup. That kindergarten boy who visited me in the Naval
hospital is now a twenty-year-old man, a junior in college.
This morning he sent me a picture of eggs Benedict that
he made from scratch all on his own (including the English
muffin and hollandaise sauce). He loves to run and is very
organized, self-motivated, and self-aware. He writes me short
stories for Mother's Day and never forgets my birthday. He
inherited my anxiety, but he's really good at facing his fears.
He's so different than who I was at his age. We never did get
to live together again, but we had many visits, as often as
distance would allow. In the beginning, I sucked at getting
child support to his dad on time, but once I was more stable,
I never missed a payment.

Today, one of my favorite things is having conversations
with him about the latest superhero movie or current events.
We are mother and son and we have been in our own little way
since the beginning.

There is life after rock bottom—no matter how hard or far
we have gone—and it is big and rich and hard and beautiful!
When we are no longer weighed down by the burdens of all our
painful baggage, we become aware of our true nature, our beautiful internal voice, and the wings that intuition gives us. We're
free to fly.

STEP SEVEN PRACTICE:
The Tree of Self-Acceptance

Open your journal to a new page or get out a piece of water-color paper and make your own tree of self-acceptance.

1. Fold your paper in half or open your journal so you have two blank pages, side by side. Start with the background. You can paint it with watercolor, choose a fun paper, or draw/color it with markers.

2. On the left side, draw, paint, write, or glue pictures of things that represent your true self; on the right, draw, paint, write, or glue pictures of everything you've collected over the years that makes you who you are today. Include EVERYTHING you think makes you who you are. Don't want to make a tree specifically? That's fine. Make it abstract or a collage or even a meadow.

3. As you progress, start to blend the two together at the crease by painting over the middle line and seeing how the colors mix. Notice how you felt while creating. How do you feel after you've created? Can you find beauty in both sides? If not, add something beautiful. THAT IS YOU NOW.

CHAPTER EIGHT

Self-Expression Is a Form of Intuition

Mama sat across from me at the supper table as I prattled on about my latest obsession. I was in the process of training for a full marathon, and if you've ever trained for a full marathon, you know it's just about all that you can talk about during that season. Mama stared back at me as I talked about carbs and long runs and rest days with an almost confused expression, "It's like you've changed your DNA completely."

In a way, she was right. Years earlier, during the shock therapy treatments that helped me survive and even before that, I was a chain smoker and former binge drinker. I wasn't able to keep my living room clean or pay my bills on time; even getting the mail seemed like an impossible task. So, I guess I could see how she thought New Maggie might have changed her DNA. I had truly become a different person.

As I've mentioned, butterflies are my favorite metaphor. A caterpillar goes along through life, crawling on the ground and on leaves, happy enough, maybe a bit hungry. And then all of a sudden, all of life's messages are telling her that it's time to go, that a change is coming. So, she instinctively stops and forms a chrysalis from her own body. Her caterpillar body dies, gets digested, and turns to goop. And the wisdom of her creation transforms her into the butterfly, using all the sludge to build wings. She can't be forced out too soon. The struggle to emerge from the chrysalis pumps vital nutrients into her wings so she can fly. Her wings need the struggle. And when she's finally out of her shell, she has to hang out for a bit while her wings dry, perhaps like a meditation, rest, or reflection period. And then she gets the message, "Time to fly." And off she goes spreading her wings. It's not overnight and it's not bubble baths and candles.

She all but completely changed her DNA. And that shit was hard. It was exhausting. Self-expression usually is.

SELF-EXPRESSION STARTS WITH INTUITION

Recovery taught me that I had to clean up my side of the street. I had to clear out a channel to my innermost self, so that my HP could get through. The caterpillar of my old life had to be digested and discarded, but I had to be able to hear the calling inside me to know when it was time to change—or else I might die. All the junk had to be swept out through contemplation and self-examination. When I cleared out the buildup of stuff that didn't belong to me, I had room for new ideas. I could get to know me and what it was that I want to put forth into the world.

How did I do that? By inventory. Without keeping track of what's going in and coming out, a business will go bankrupt. If we are not in tune with ourselves, with what we're putting into our bodies and minds, what we're believing about ourselves and others, then we are going to be numb, and probably, restless, irritable, and discontent.

We are meant to express ourselves. And we are meant to express ourselves truthfully.

For years, my favorite self-expression was fitness. I loved running and lifting weights and making and meeting goals from weight lost to weight lifted. When I committed to something, I trained hard for it, whether it was a half-marathon or a jiujitsu class. I overly identified with this part of my personality. Every social media post was about it. I devoted years to a fitness-related MLM (multi-level marketing, often referred to as pyramid schemes) and devoted A LOT of time to sharing about my journey.

But behind the scenes, I was struggling with binge eating and under-eating and overexercising. My goals were getting harder to meet as I became harder and harder on myself. I gave up dieting and weighing myself and started to go to twelve-step meetings dedicated to these behaviors and finally began to look at that part of myself. It was time for another transformation.

YOUR SUPERPOWER IS YOUR INTUITION

The best way to learn how to stay on the path is to get off the path. I didn't learn my true values until I took actions that were not in line with my true values. We learn very young not to touch the hot stove because of the loud grown-ups telling us not to touch the hot stove, or even better, we learn the lesson by touching the hot stove. That is in our tool kit now: stove hot equals don't touch. When we take actions that aren't safe for our soul or out of line with our beliefs, we'll get a similar scorching sensation, but in our bellies or our throats. If we're listening to what our body is telling us, what our soul is telling us, then we can use that pain to guide us back to our values and our true path.

Intuition is a muscle we strengthen when we know and accept who we are. For as long as I can remember, I didn't trust my intuition. The voices outside of me were much louder than the voice inside of me. My fear and anxiety were also much louder than that still small voice. I trusted what everyone else was doing far more than I trusted myself. Most of my life, I felt alone and like I didn't belong. I wanted to fit in so badly that I overrode my internal compass. I didn't trust myself enough to make my own decisions. I chose my first career from this place. I joined the military, which was a really good fit because I was told where to be, at what time (five minutes early is late), in what uniform, and exactly how my bed should be made before I left to go there. And when I got to work, I had a binder of instructions telling me exactly what to do next. I didn't need intuition; I had the US Navy.

But like my DNA, over time, that changed, as I began to strengthen my intuition muscle. And the more I got to know myself, the more I was able to believe that tiny voice inside. Today, my intuition is so strong it sometimes feels like a psychic power. I feel my husband's energy and know whether or not to make a silly joke about the lint stuck to his hair. I feel Mason's energy and can usually tell when he's going to spike a temperature. I feel Clayton's anxiety when they're unsure about school or when they've told a lie. I just know. I don't know how I know, but I know. I feel clearly whether or not I can trust a person from the very first moment I meet them. If they set off my Spidey-sense, it will be hard for me to ever trust them, even if I don't know why. The times I've chosen to ignore this super-power, I've regretted not heeding the message. Maybe it's just intuition or insight that comes from years of self-examination (stillness and contemplation) and paying attention. Maybe it's the hypervigilance that I learned as a child with anxiety and fear. But now, I would consider being a highly sensitive and feeling person to be a superpower and one I would never want to give up.

A famous Gandhi quote goes, "Happiness is when what you think, what you say, and what you do are in harmony." That is the gift of growing our intuition.

SELF-EXPRESSION STARTS
WITH COMMUNITY

Our home and our family—whether biological or chosen—are like the outer shell of a chrysalis. They surround us and love us during the times when we must rebuild ourselves, whether it's a mental health day or a year of unraveling. Our community is the tree branch that holds our chrysalis, allowing our transformation to happen. It's where we can do our best work—mothering; nurturing ourselves, our children, our students, and our friends; holding space for those around us and setting boundaries for ourselves.

Which is how I became a teacher by accident.

One day, I was given some flyers while waiting in the elementary school car pickup line. Since there was candy attached, I sort of tossed it in the back seat to my child, and was like, "Here you take this, there's candy." I didn't even read the flyer, but Clayton did, replying, "Hey, Mom! You should be a teacher! They need substitute teachers!"

I gave the noncommittal "We'll see" that every parent knows means "Most likely, we won't see," but a seed was planted. I talked it over with Nick and he sort of shrugged and said, "It might be good for you to get out of the house."

I took a very long time to finish my application, and then summer came, but when school started back, so did I. I got to teach that first week of school. And I loved it immediately. The kids responded pretty well, and if anything, they enjoyed hearing my sea stories and playing "Would You Rather" in between read-alouds or worksheets. Other teachers started telling me that I should become a teacher officially. I ignored them because I was writing a book and wanted flexibility. Then a math teacher position opened up and the timing was just too good. My intuition told me that this was supposed to happen. The kids I've connected with and the teachers I get to work with are the huge gifts from following that intuition. I never in a gazillion years thought my path would wind through sixth-grade math class, but here we are. I'm going to stay here until it's time to move on to the next right thing, while trusting that intuition and celebrating the 3 Things along the way.

Teaching isn't the only way that I have connected my creativity to community. When I reclaimed my artist within, photos of my watercolor doodles took the place of those old post-workout selfies. I shared my progress with my online community, and the encouragement and feedback I received fed the process. I committed to a watercolor painting a day, shared my progress, and had friends online do the same. My love of fitness goals and commitments had transferred over to my art.

I started a writing circle in my hometown. For the past couple of years, I had been part of a writing community where we met online to talk about our writing struggles and victories. That community witnessed this book coming to fruition. I connected with folks in my town who were writing, or wanted to write, so I started an in-person writing group. Talking about writing is such a beautiful way to honor the writer in us all.

A local potter holds workshops in town. I absolutely love it when she does. Not only do I get to create, but I get to do it with my community. I feel the same way about those paint parties or studios. I love creating art with others.

My sister is an amazing party planner. She was Pinterest perfection before there was Pinterest. It's a hobby that blesses all of us who get to attend her parties. Her creativity wows her guests every time, and she sets the scene for beautiful fellowship. She got it from my grandmama, who threw elaborate parties for her community at Christmas. My cousin Bessie got the gene, too; she can throw a beautifully planned barbecue that could grace the cover of a magazine.

On a smaller level, I enjoy simple entertaining in my home. Using my creativity, alongside my partner, to be in community with our friends and family over a meal and sharing stories.

FINDING THE CREATOR WITHIN

I spent years identifying as "not an artist" and "not a writer"—this mentality not only destroyed my creativity, but it also disconnected me from my intuition, which yearned for me to create. How strongly we hold on to these "anti-" identities.

After getting sick with COVID, I went from running half marathons to being essentially bedridden. I couldn't walk to the kitchen without feeling faint and out of breath. There were nights that I cried myself to sleep, not knowing if I would wake up the next day. In what felt like overnight, I gained fifty pounds, and I grieved the version of me that was an athlete.

I had lost my identity. It was time to go inward, another chrysalis. I reclaimed the writer and the artist in me, listening, even through the pain, to that small, still voice of my intuition: "Create."

So, instead of running a marathon, I bought a watercolor kit. I'd always wanted to learn how to paint watercolors, and everyone was trying new things at home during the spring of 2020. I didn't learn to bake bread, but I did finally learn watercolors.

Showing up every day for my watercolors and morning journaling sowed my creative garden so I could plant the seed of this book. The act of committing to this book folded me into a whole community of online writers, many of whom I've never met in person. Slowly the voice that yelled, "I'm not a writer," was drowned out by my writing coach giving feedback and saying things like, "People who aren't writers don't show up to writing groups on a Sunday afternoon," and, "If you write, you are a writer," and "People who aren't writers never think about whether or not they are a writer." I would have quit almost immediately had it not been for my writing family.

When I first joined the group, it was literally painful for me to read my words out loud. Opening myself up to feedback was almost unbearable. That sounds dramatic, I know, but the only way for me to become an empowered creative was to show up scared half to death, voice trembling, praying that my Wi-Fi would go out before my turn. But I kept showing up. Not only did I grow and improve, but I got to listen to others read their work, which was just as powerful as being heard.

The little Maggie who carried her sketchbook everywhere knew that I was a creator. I've been a creator all along.

> All I had to do was remember: I am an artist. I am a writer. I am a creator. We all are. And we prove it by showing up on the page and in the communities of artists around us.

One of my favorite recovery mantras is "Do the next right thing." I've heard this in twelve-step rooms for years and I know Glennon Doyle says it, too (either way, not mine to take credit for). When I'm not at all sure what my next move should be, I ask myself, What is the next right thing? Usually, it's something like go make lunch, or take your meds, or get dressed. Something very simple. Most of the time there aren't earth-shattering consequences to our next decision, but when we're living true to ourselves, it all adds up over time to GOOD.

One of the hardest parts of this recovery stuff is that even though I have a community and I'm not alone, no one is going to do it for me. Only we, alone, can do the deep internal work. My sponsor always leads her advice with "I'm not gonna tell you what to do" and then she shares her applicable experience, strength, and hope. She says that because ultimately the next right thing is my choice.

We can't rest for each other, we can't heal for each other, and we can't choose for each other, but we can hold space and be kind and do the next right thing to support one another.

Holding space for each other, that's the good stuff about connection. When we build that muscle of intuition, we reach a new level of self-realization. We learn to do the next right thing in our own homes and communities, in our daily routines, and in the callings of life. All of this leads to the celebration of "Glorifying God." I know, I know, the G-word. But I promise, it's not what you think.

STEP EIGHT PRACTICE:
AEIOU (and Always Y)

I first learned this practice from an Overeaters Anonymous (OA) meeting podcast and later, I read it in Brené Brown's *The Gifts of Imperfection*. I use it with my sponsees (the people that I mentor in recovery) and with my sponsor as a daily check-in and inventory.

Here is my own version of the AEIOU check-in and how I have adapted it:

1. Find an accountability partner—someone who supports you in your adventure of collective recovery and would be willing to do this work with you.

2. Pick a time each day (morning, lunch break, or before bed) to text each other the following:

A (*abstinence/accountability*): In OA, I would write how I was doing with food that day. When I use this practice with those in alcohol recovery, we talk about cravings, emotional sobriety, and when our next meeting will be. You can use it for whatever you most need to be held accountable.

E (*exercise*): You get to define what exercise is for you. I am most connected to my creativity and my HP when I get at least thirty minutes of movement a day, whether it's walking, running, yoga, or Zumba.

I ("What have *I* done for myself today?"): For me, this is my self-care practices or setting a boundary, saying no or yes to something new, recovery time, etc.

O ("What have I done for *others* today?"): This is great in getting me out of myself and my own problems. I will admit that as a full-time teacher and parent, a lot of times my O is just me gesturing with my hands as if to say, "All of this."

U (*unresolved* emotions): What is uncomfortable right now?

Y (*Yippee, yay! Yahoo!*): This is where we focus on what we are grateful for.

Here is an example of one of my AEIOUs:

A—Feeling pretty good today, connected with HP outside in the sun, planning on hitting a Zoom meeting later.

E—I could really use a good sweat session . . . tbd.

I—Took a glorious nap and now I'm enjoying writing.

O—Took time to engage with the boys on their gaming convos.

U—My car wouldn't start today. Trying not to catastrophize, or future trip, or hyperfocus on car shopping.

Y—One week left of school! Woo-hoo!

Now, try out your own!

PART THREE

Glorify God in All That You Do

I make a point to appreciate all the little things in my life. I go out and smell the air after a good, hard rain. These small actions help remind me that there are so many great, glorious pieces of good in the world.

—Dolly Parton

CHAPTER NINE

What Is God?

Here we are—either the moment you've been waiting for or the moment you've been skeptical about. We're going to talk about *the God thing*. This is not a Christian book. This is about whatever your HP looks like. If you practice a religion, it applies here! If you don't practice a religion or are atheist, that also applies here!

I was born and raised an Episcopalian, my daddy was a priest, his daddy was a priest. We went to church every Sunday. I complained A LOT about church when I was a preteen, but I went. When my siblings and I were a little bit older, we had the choice to go or stay home, and I went even then (and usually hungover). I went because I felt the community there and I also believed I needed to go atone for my sins that no one else knew about.

Church was where our community was. There was the occasional drama, but mostly we had the coolest church family around, so I was pretty eager to attend. I loved the music and the smells and the ritual and the routines. I loved the calendar and the different colors on the altar throughout the year. I really loved communion (I chose to stop taking communion after I got sober, but that was a personal choice based solely on the fact that I just loved it way too much). There were times when I was brought to tears over a song or a sermon (the 3 Things!); weddings always made me cry, and of course, so did funerals. We rejoiced in the happy times, like baptisms and celebrations. But I can't say for sure if I ever felt God or Jesus in any of it.

If anything, I felt like I wasn't doing it right. I figured there must be something wrong with me because I felt such guilt, shame, and lack of belonging on the inside. I watched all of these people, smiling and happy and praying and singing, and I just didn't know how to tap into whatever magical Jesus powers they had.

I also went to other churches with friends over the years. Before moving to South Florida, Daddy's first church was in southern Georgia. Most of my friends were Southern Baptist— they were actually quite suspicious of Episcopalians, and I'm pretty sure some even thought we worshiped the devil. One time, I went to church with a bestie and the preacher asked people to come up to the front if they wanted to ask Jesus into their hearts and be saved. Well, I mean, hell yes, I wanted to be saved. I wasn't sure what this meant, but if I got to go to the front and get clapped for *and* they would teach me to be friends with Jesus, then let's do this! I went up there and they just said a prayer. And then they had me say, "I accept Jesus into my heart," and that was it.

I didn't feel any different. If anything, I felt like a faker because Jesus did not magically appear in my heart. But I would go on to be saved with three other friends in three different churches because I loved the attention, and hell, it couldn't hurt, right? I was secretly hoping one of them would take.

Some believe you have to accept Jesus into your heart for salvation, some believe you need to be baptized, and others believe that we were saved when Jesus died on the cross. I can't wrap my head around the idea that I was "saved" by the torture and murder of a prophet, which is why this isn't a Christian book. Because for all those fake deliverances, I never truly believed in JC as my personal savior.

This really ate at me as the child of a priest living my dual Maggie life as a teenager. I would feel moments where I was moved to tears—Daddy calls them close moments—times where I can say now as an adult that my HP was stirring in me. The emotion was a gift, a chance to feel something larger than myself. Those close moments allowed me to feel the belonging of the community of the church, of the family, and if you be-lieve in it, the presence of a spiritual being. They came with goose bumps and chills and were really beautiful, but then they would leave, and I would be left with doubt and teenage hor-monal mood swings again. No matter how good those God shots were, I preferred the kind with booze. So, after church, I would go out and binge drink and do whatever the hell I want-ed to do with whoever the hell I wanted to do it with.

But I rarely blew my cover as the good kid. I was an acolyte (essentially an altar girl). I loved it when I was allowed to do the scripture readings in front of the church. I found joy in public speaking. I craved the smells and routine. As part of the youth group community in our diocese (region of the church), I got to lead a Happening weekend (basically like a retreat or conference for teens). They let me pick the theme for the weekend, and I chose "Pour Out Your Spirit in This Place" because I experienced one of those close moments in church when we sang the song:

> *Pour out Your Spirit in this place*
> *That we might see Your power*
> *And we might feel Your grace.*

This was a prayer for me. I wanted to see the power and feel the grace so I could know that God was real and that there wasn't something wrong with me. Plus, when I sang the song in a room with other people, I felt those close moments. There was a portion of the program where the attendees got their feet washed by the team to symbolize being made clean, the forgiveness of sins, and the humility and kindness that Jesus showed. I was okay with the intimacy of washing feet. It was an honor to be able to wash the feet of my friends in such a humbling way. But then it was my turn to have my feet washed by my daddy, I lost it and was a blubbering mess. I didn't feel worthy of having my feet washed. I realized in that instance that I did not feel worthy of Jesus's or God's love, and maybe that's why the close moments never lasted; maybe that's why I never felt "saved."

What was wrong with me, why wasn't I getting the message, and why wasn't I getting saved from myself?

I didn't believe I was worthy.

I wrestled for a long time with the God thing. I had many questions and no answers. But then I began to realize, I didn't need to find God in order to believe in God. I just needed to feel something, anything, the little flash that there was something out there bigger than me.

And I got to decide what that thing was.

REDEFINING GOD
(NO BIGGIE, Y'ALL)

Walking into Holy Spirit Episcopal Church for the first time after deployment was a bit surreal. I was wearing my crackerjacks—the name of the white dress uniform worn for important occasions such as this. I wouldn't be caught dead in a Navy town in my dress uniform, but in West Palm Beach, going home in my whites felt poetic after being deployed during 9/11. I walked into the familiar smell—the mix of shadow frankincense from a Christmas past and the scent of new carpet, the sounds of laughter and voices, my family. There were so many new and diverse faces.

Most of the churches we'd attended were comprised of mainly white people, but this church that had been my home for so long, and still kind of was, had grown into something far more beautiful. There were Black families and Haitian families and families with two moms, families with two dads. And there was his booming voice, "Welcome to Holy Spirit, where all are welcome. You are home."

You are home. I am home.

And we don't need to find it in church, but in order to stand in collective recovery, we need to find the light somewhere. We need to find a place we can call home.

It's okay to give ourselves permission to move away from what we were taught and redefine what God means to us. What does that look like? For a while, it meant I didn't go to church at all. We joke now that Daddy ruined church for me, and I agree that that's partly true—I still have not found a church like Holy Spirit Episcopal Church. There hasn't been one as inclusive or welcoming or that felt as much like a family since. (I'm sad to say, five years after my dad's retirement, Holy Spirit Episcopal Church had to close its doors for good this past year due to the pandemic and ongoing financial issues. It was the end of a beautiful era.)

When I got into twelve-step recovery, they talked about this idea of "choosing your own conception of God." Even with my open-minded upbringing, I balked at this. It felt blasphemous and wrong. Like I can't imagine what God is—God is God. It's already been defined in all the books and by all the churches; we've seen what he looks like in the paintings and sculptures. Who am I to choose what God is?

Okay, so let's have some real talk. While many believe that the Bible is the word of God, it was written by man. The images in stained glass windows and on ceilings in chapels are painted by humans—conceived in the brains of people like you and me. It's their conception of God. So why can't I come up with a conception of God that works for me in my life? Thunderbolt-hell-and-brimstone God doesn't work in my life. Man in the clouds doesn't work in my life. A God that excludes people because of who they love doesn't work in my life. Blond hair, blue-eyed Jesus doesn't work in my life. Over time, my twelve-step recovery taught me to find my own conception of God, who I call HP or the Universe, usually just HP.

I knew all the things my HP wasn't, but it took me a while to define what my HP was. And to make it even more confusing, I still can't ever completely define this thing—but having a beginning concept helps.

My first sponsor, Linda, told me that if I wasn't ready or couldn't figure out my own conception, or if mine wasn't working, I could borrow hers. She was sober and happy and sane, so I believed what she believed. When I prayed, I pictured the little framed picture of the virgin mother she had over her chair where we worked the steps, and I talked to Linda's HP. And for a while that worked. In seeking my version of God, I tried different churches, and I changed sponsors and borrowed other people's HPs.

And then I kept going. I tried more churches. I listened in meetings and took bits and pieces here and there. I read books, so many books. After all, I was an information collector. Well, that applied to trying to define my HP too. I feel like I was late to the podcast game, but during a time of seeking, I finally asked a friend to tell me what they were and how to find them. She patiently explained exactly how to download an app and recommended several to try. This was at a time when I was on a spiritual deep dive (I got tired of being a water bug, skimming on the surface) and I was all over her recommendation for Oprah's podcast.

I can still see myself standing in the middle of my kitchen when I heard an episode with an Episcopal priest, Reverend Ed

Bacon. He spoke of grace and activism, and of being a child growing up in southern Georgia . . . and I froze! This wasn't just a wise speaker on my favorite podcast, this was *my* Ed. The Ed Bacon that was present at my parents' wedding and my birth and the death of Jacob, my twin, and who blessed my aunt and uncle's haunted house. This was the same Ed whom my grandmama took credit for praying into the Episcopal church after being a Baptist minister. Ed has since been a prayer warrior for my family. He was a spiritual guide during my brain tumor journey, and I even interviewed him for this book, back when I thought it was going to be a collection of other people's stories, rather than my own.

That day in my kitchen on my podcast binge, Ed defined my HP almost perfectly. He said the theologian Thomas Merton talks of God as the True Self. That blew me away because in my meditation when I get still, I have this sense that my HP is at my core. At first, I was conflicted when I noticed these sensations. My earliest conceptions of an HP had been this sort of "God in the clouds" entity thing. I would direct my prayers upward and outward and I would hear them in my ear, and they would fall flat. When I started praying and writing to that still place inside me, I started building a relationship with my HP. Being true to myself helped me find my HP. I discovered that my HP is inside me, God is inside me as my higher self. It's the same God that is in all of us, that thread of the divine that each of us can tap into if we get quiet enough.

I don't need to find God to feel God, I just need to seek God. And I am a seeker. Always have been. Seeker of pleasure. Seeker of attention. Seeker of knowledge. And now, a seeker of faith. I collected all these bits and pieces of what I think my HP is and every time I would think I had it defined, I would hit a bottom. Then, one day, I heard the song "Let the Mystery Be" by Iris Dement. The lyrics, especially the last verse, gave me so much comfort.

It healed the need to define in words what my HP is and left me to define my HP in feeling:

> *Some say they're goin' to a place called Glory*
> *And I ain't saying it ain't a fact*
> *But I've heard that I'm on the road to purgatory*
> *And I don't like the sound of that*
> *I believe in love and I live my life accordingly*
> *But I choose to let the mystery be.*

This need for certainty and to have others believe in that certainty too made me really uncomfortable and confused. I knew what my God wasn't. My God wasn't exclusionary. My HP wasn't gendered or American or any one human being or any one religion.

And I decided I was okay with letting the mystery be.

SPIRITUAL, NOT RELIGIOUS

There's an old Daniel Tosh joke (I know, I know, that guy's more problematic than God) where a girl says, "I'm not religious, I'm spiritual," and he says, "I'm not honest, but you're interesting."

But spirituality isn't religiosity. For some, spiritual awakenings take place like a lightning bolt. But my moment of transformation happened in stages, like the peeling of a beautiful and sacred and painful onion. I just had to open myself up to the idea that maybe there was a power greater than me and that maybe I could be restored to sanity. There was proof around me after all. These smiling happy drunks with stories filled with tragedy had come back from the brink and were now living happy, joyous, and free. As it turns out, my problem wasn't that I didn't believe in a power greater than me; it was that I didn't believe I was worthy of that power restoring me to sanity.

I chose to call God my HP because the word "God" comes with so much baggage and boxes (like Daniel Tosh jokes). Because God is just a placeholder to me. My HP can't be put into a manmade box, and sometimes I don't even believe in God at all. I doubt everything regularly, but I can look up and see the sky. I've heard many different definitions of God in the recovery rooms. For some, God stands for Great OutDoors. For others, it's Group Of Drunks. I've also heard Good Orderly Direction. Sometimes I call my HP Gus (Great Universal Spirit). I can feel my heartbeat and my breath. I am not doing that shit. I am not controlling my heartbeat. Something greater than Maggie is doing that. Science, electricity, anatomy, whatever you'd like to call it. I depend on it to survive, and yet, I can't see it. I see evidence of it, I trust that it's there, and then sometimes still, I doubt that it's there at all.

> Belief is big and strong and robust. But so is doubt. I would say that faith and doubt are always in direct correlation.

Maybe you don't have this wishy-washy faith like I do. There's a lot I don't know. But what I do know is that I am a human being who has a divine thread running through me. However, this is still very much a human existence—and sometimes, it's hard to remember the divine part. It takes work for me to counter this core belief in me that I don't belong.

I'm not sure where the core belief started. It could have come from the moment of my birth, when my mother lost her other baby and was steeped in grief. Having a depressed mama on your birthday every year, through no fault of her own, sends its own sad messages. Maybe I had survivor guilt. Every time I started in a new school or new program or camp or job or the Navy or got sober or went vegan or got tattoos or made the decision to leave or stood up for myself, I always felt uncomfortable, I always felt out of place.

In her book *Braving the Wilderness*, Brené Brown says, "Stop walking through the world looking for confirmation that you don't belong. You will always find it because you've made that your mission. Stop scouring people's faces for evidence that you're not enough. You will always find it because you've made that your goal."

After I heard this quote, I scoured all of Brené's books for her work on belonging. Challenging this core belief was key in order for me to have a relationship with an HP, to truly accept myself, and to be able to glorify God in all that I do. Because I was walking through the world looking for proof that I didn't belong, and I was tired of finding it.

. . .

When I turned thirty-nine, I took myself on my first yoga birthday retreat, heading to an Ashram outside of Charlottesville, Virginia, called Satchidananda, also called Yogaville. They offer Integral Yoga training as well as yoga retreats and personal retreats. It was my first real immersion into yoga as a practice and not "Westernized" yoga. I was really in over my head. I knew I was on sacred ground from the moment I arrived. There was a mid-day trip to the LOTUS (Light of Truth Universal Shrine) temple each day that was optional, but it was suggested that we attend at least once while we were there.

The temple was a bit of a hike (or van ride) so some chose to nap during that time, but I was committed to cramming all the conscious contact that I could into this retreat (ever the recovering perfectionist!). I was actually getting quite frantic because I was afraid I would miss the moment that was going to help me with my lack of belonging. I was afraid I wouldn't learn the thing I needed to learn to get me on the right path, to show me the teacher I needed, or the lesson I required so I could find my HP. I am a very determined seeker.

Our teacher, Durga Leela, kept asking us to go back to one question, What is our heart's desire? My answer was the same every time: TRUE BELONGING.

I went to the LOTUS temple with a van full of recovery people, already feeling like a family. Of course, I still felt like they all knew what they were doing, and I didn't, and at any moment, I'd be told that I was doing it wrong and that I needed to leave. It felt like everyone else knew where to go, where to put their shoes, the right way to enter the temple (which apparently was to go in on the left). I fumbled along behind everyone, self-conscious and hoping I didn't appear to be as much of a spiritual fledgling as I felt.

Walking up the left sidewalk to the LOTUS temple, I will never forget the awe I felt. The building is bright pink and blue and quite literally the shape of a lotus blossom. There are fountains along the pathway, and I felt an undeniable sacred feeling as I approached the shrine. Entering the temple, we were to leave our shoes outside the door, grab a cushion, and find a spot inside before the ceremony began. Every religion is represented inside the temple.

I found my spot and I got comfortable, and as the meditation proceeded, I remember feeling the dialogue, *I suck at this, I'll never get quiet, they're all better than me, what if I fart, oh god was that my stomach* . . . and then something happened. I felt my body. I felt the space inside my body and my breath, and I started to process the word "belonging" and the desire I had found during the morning meditation.

The longing to belong ached inside my body.

The still space I fell into revealed that I already belonged. I belong to me. I belong to my family. I belong to my HP. Each human being, and each sentient being, has that space within them as well, and to that space in them, I also belong.

I had a vision of being at peace the way you are at the bottom of a busy swimming pool where the top is agitated, but down below, it's calm and quiet. I sat in the calm, and I belonged. And that's when I realized that I could go to the retreats, I could attend church, I could listen to the podcasts, or read the books, but God, or HP, or GUS, magically, miraculously, always lived within me. And it lives within you too.

STEP NINE PRACTICE:
The God Thing

We need to talk about the God Thing. For your HP to work with you, it's important to have a concept of God that works for you. This exercise will help you do just that. At a minimum you'll find out what your HP is NOT, which is half the battle.

1. Draw a line down the center of one of your journal pages.
2. Label one side "MY HIGHER POWER IS . . ." and label the other side "MY HIGHER POWER IS NOT . . ." Don't skimp on these lists; try to fill the page. (Remember, you don't have to believe in a God to do this exercise. HP can be defined as a power greater than ourselves. (Love, community, nature—all of these can be on your list.)
3. If you get stuck, answer the following questions:

What do the people who raised you call their HP? Does that work for you?

What has given you strength during hard times in your past?

What is your deepest desire?

When do you feel most peaceful?

When do you feel like you have it most together?

4. Meditate for a few minutes and write down any other thoughts that come to mind.
5. After you've written your lists, turn to a fresh page in your art journal or get out a piece of watercolor paper. Paint or collage all the feelings your HP list gives you.

When you are in moments of doubt or indecision, remember your list and your painting, and trust that there is a power greater than you that you can turn to and plug into in times of need.

CHAPTER TEN

God Is a Creative,
and So Are We

For those among us who believe in God, it's not a stretch to see God as a Creator. And many believe that we are created in God's image. And if we were fashioned after the Ultimate Creator, then it would follow that we're inherently creative. We were designed with the need, the instinct, the desire to express our creativity. If intuition is a gift from our HP, then the journey through the 3 Things is about creativity. It's in all that we do, from picking out our work clothes to how we'll get the Christmas card thing pulled off this year (spoiler: I probably won't). It's more easily noticed in the times of "I wish I had a camera to capture this moment" or "I should write this down" or "I bet I could draw something like that" or "This could use more thyme."

Grandmother started using watercolors soon after Grandfather died. He went out for a run in May 1994 and never came back. Her grief was profound, and her HP guided her to connect with this new art form as a way to find herself after losing her mate. She was always an artist. She dyed her own wool and spun it into beautiful yarn, and she had many looms that she used in her art. But after this life change, she took up painting and calligraphy and she made cards and bookmarks for everyone.

I started watercolors after my own profound grief in dealing with chronic health issues that led to finding my brain tumor. Grandmother's supplies were sitting in my parents' storage, and I was invited to go through them to see what I could use. The feeling of living into my path, my purpose had never been so strong as when I sorted through her art supplies. I was touching her paper and paints, and the ideas came one after another. I felt as if electricity was pulsing through my fingertips.

Before I started my recovery, and well into sobriety, I told anyone who would listen that I didn't have a creative bone in my body. I wrote poems, I painted watercolors, you already heard about the cake, and yet, I didn't have a creative bone in my body? It wasn't until recently, when a friend essentially grabbed my face and yelled at me, "You are an artist, damn it!" that I allowed myself to explore what being an artist meant.

My whole life, I lived with this old idea that you had to have a master's degree in fine arts or years of training to call yourself an artist or a writer—but here I am writing this book, with art exercises included. The more I create, the more I see things through the eyes of an artist. Colors are brighter. I have thoughts like *Ooh, I should paint that* or *Give me a pen, I need to write that down.*

We are all artists. That's why all children are creative. Because we are all a part of creation. And let's face it, life is more beautiful, more meaningful when we get to be a part of the creation. When we start seeing everything as an opportunity for creativity, the mundane becomes miraculous. From packing lunches to teaching math lessons to twelve-year-olds, all of this is how we share our gifts with others, how we glorify God (however we define that) in all that we do.

SEEKING OUR CREATIVITY

If God is creativity and we are spiritually seeking a power greater than ourselves—or higher thinking, higher consciousness, enlightenment—wouldn't that mean we are seeking creativity? Being open to an HP opens us up to creating, whether it's high art, making music in our spare time, party planning for our kids, or making the perfect omelet or the most extra spreadsheet.

> Seeking creativity comes from being true to ourselves because our true selves are creative by nature.

It may not feel that way at first, but when we get quiet day after day and tap into that deeper intuition, magic begins to happen, and creativity naturally begins to flow.

For me, one of the hardest parts of adulthood is the lie that we know everything; that everything is certain. As we age, we become experts on this thing or that thing, but we fail to remember what it's like to not know about the thing in which we're experts—or even more importantly, in which we are not experts. If we know all there is to know, then why ask questions or learn anything new? This way of thinking steals our creativity and our childlike curiosity.

The perfect recipe for killing all imagination and progress is "This is how we've always done it." I try to remind myself to hold on to that childlike curiosity—the one of cloud watching and the sometimes-incessant *whys*. Children are the best question-askers until they start to care more about what others think of them than the wonders of this beautiful existence.

Art is the outward expression of our Universal gift of creativity. They say beauty is in the eye of the beholder, but art is the soul of the creator. It is unique to each of us, and while some value their ability to identify and critique works of art, it's all up to the creator. I have spent years denying that I am creative, but the 3 Things have taught me that I am creative simply because I exist.

When I recovered the artist within me, through practicing my creativity, I stopped denying. It has reached all areas of my life. I am no longer willing to sit in my problems for very long, I'm motivated to seek out creative solutions.

DISCOVERING OUR CREATIVITY

Let's challenge the old ideas that we have about what it means to be creative. Creativity is making something new out of the old. It's trying new ways of doing things. We connect to our creativity by using our gifts and talents—and doing the next right thing. Yes, artists use their creativity to make art. Teachers use their creativity to teach. Healers use their creativity to heal.

An amazing example of "I am creative because I exist" is Jesus! Jesus was a creative. He was a carpenter. Scripture says that he was a healer and a miracle worker and a prophet. He was also a teacher. The first line of the Bible says, "In the beginning God created the heavens and the Earth," and if we believe that Jesus is God and God is Jesus, well then, Jesus is the Ultimate Creator.

I can't speak of Jesus with any sort of certainty without having questions pop up. It's too big for my small human head to wrap around. And my logical brain fails to suspend my own disbelief around much of what is written of Jesus and the supernatural acts surrounding his story. Don't get me wrong. I love the idea of Jesus. I find the red letters in the Bible to be generally wonderful teachings. (For the non-Christians among us, certain versions of the New Testament in the Bible have Jesus's teachings in red print.)

But I don't think he would be happy with how his followers are using scripture as weapons and shields from accountability, picking and choosing which verses will support their limited worldview and leaving out the parts that don't. The famous WWJD (What Would Jesus Do) should be changed to WWJAD (What Would Jesus Actually Do).

The Jesus I want to follow is the table-flipping Jesus. The Jesus that loved the outcasts and the sinners. The Jesus I want to follow fed the multitudes and warned against greed and hoarding possessions.

WWJAD? He would feed and house and minister to the masses unconditionally, and he would fight for things like living wages for all and taxing the rich. I want to be like the hands and feet of Jesus here on earth, teaching and creating and calling for change. Boy, does that take creativity!

I am creative because I exist. Does that feel like a leap? It might. But once we acknowledge that, we can see all the ways that we are creatives, tapping into the creative source within us. How can we ALL connect to our creativity? Making dinner, writing lesson plans, working in the garden—these mundane tasks are creativity. Living into our purpose is creativity, especially when it doesn't make logical sense. (Me? A teacher? What?)

GLORIFYING OUR CREATIVITY

For the first half of my sobriety, I felt like I was praying to nothing. I'm a really good rule follower, despite the double life of my youth, and I wanted to do what I was told. I would picture God in the clouds or my dad's big ol' gigantic hands in the sky. I didn't understand what meditation meant either. The Big Book intentionally left this vague so that each member could find what worked for them personally, but man, early on, I struggled with it.

So, I decided to start writing my prayers in my morning journal practice. Rather than talking to the God in the clouds, I found that my arm and my pen are a direct connection to that still place within me. This practice is where I connect directly to my HP. My prayers are letters to God, and if I move my pen long enough and without my ego mind interrupting too much, then I find that my prayers also get answered either directly from the pen as organized thoughts or insights, or later in my day or week or year. Or they work themselves out on the page.

During my journey with Julia Cameron's *The Artist's Way*, there was an assignment to write my own artist's prayer. I started reading this prayer after my morning pages to round off my practice and start my day. Here is the prayer I came up with in that process—cobbled together from wisdom I saved in my information-collecting quests and the recovery prayers I gathered over the years. It will probably evolve over time, just as I do, but this is what helped during my creative journey. You are free to use mine or create your own.

Higher Power, Creative Force,

I offer myself to life. Help me to receive the gifts of this day.

Relieve me of the bondage of self, that I might better live into what I am meant for in this world.

Help me to live in a way that is wholehearted and sound of mind.

Guide my thinking and my actions.

I surrender my old ideas and open myself to new expansive ideas.

May I approach the day with childlike curiosity, with gratitude, and a joyful heart.

Help me to have unconditional love for the human form (mine, my family, and ALL people).

Help me notice the obstacles that stand in the way of my usefulness, creativity, and connection, and help me do the next right thing until those obstacles are removed.

Allow me to use moments of defensiveness and anger as opportunities for growth and introspection.

Help me live life fully as if the Universe is friendly.

Thank you for my life, my sobriety, and my art.

Help me use this gift of a new day wisely and to glorify You in all that I do.

When I start with gratitude, everything is better. I'm training my brain to look for the things that make my life beautiful rather than all the things I lack.

Gratitude moves me from scarcity into abundance.

I see my kids at school scrambling for the best seat and the best set of markers and to be first in line. I see the fear of missing out and the fear of not getting their fair share, and I feel that in my bones. I can say there is enough for everyone all day, but that doesn't change the fact that some of these kids are fighting for survival. They are hungry and dealing with more than some of us will ever know. I can say there is enough but to them, is there?

When *all* people are valued and given space and attention, there is more than enough. Because I do have enough on a day-to-day basis, it is a sin to *not* live in gratitude and abundance. When we live in appreciation, there is less cutthroat competition because I am grateful for you and all your opportunities, and I want you to win, too! There is enough for all of us. I say that, while also knowing many among us, including some of my students, do have to fight for survival.

I will never say, "Just be grateful for what you have," or, "Focus on abundance," as a blanket statement for everyone, but I will say for me, there is nothing that gratitude will make worse.

Sitting on my writing desk is a picture of my grandmother, Daddy's mama. It's a nineties snapshot—the kind where you had to drop off the film and wait patiently for your prints. The colors have faded, but not her beautiful white hair, laugh lines, and bright smile. She smiled all the way to her twinkly eyes. Clipped to the worn edge of the photograph is her handwriting, elegantly scrawled on a scrap of paper, a quote from St. Teresa of Avila that reads, "God walks among the pots and pans."

Washing a sink full of dirty dishes, taking out the trash, chopping vegetables . . . these can all be rituals of celebration, of glorifying God, if we allow it. The closer we are to celebration in all the everyday little actions that fill our lives, the closer we are to God.

And I think Grandmother would appreciate the idea that sometimes we have to be disruptive in our celebrations. We can do the dishes AND bang the pots and pans; we can mend the blankets AND disrupt injustice; we can take out the trash AND fight for a world that honors all of us.

My husband has been a mixed martial arts fighter for years. After our kids were born, he never got back to a regular training schedule, and I could tell he was missing it. After a move to California, I encouraged him to go train for jiujitsu. He took it on and thrived with it. And soon he started recommending that I attend some classes. OH, HECK NO! Wrestling around with sweaty dudes on dirty mats did not sound fun to this introverted germophobe. Hard pass, buddy. He kept dropping suggestions. When he brought home a flyer for a women's class that didn't require a gi (the white martial arts "costume" thingy) and it was free, I hesitantly signed up. I *almost* didn't show. But I'm so glad I did.

At the free seminar, I learned a move called the trap and roll. The bad guy is on top of you, and you basically trap one of their legs and roll them off. It was magic! I went home and practiced it on my husband. From that moment on, I was hooked. I attended every class I could. I made friends. I allowed myself to show up knowing nothing—in that gi costume thingy—a true beginner. I made mistakes and let my peers and instructor guide me through them. Pretty soon I had enough skills to guide my peers who were newer than me. I started attending the co-ed class. I noticed I was walking taller outside jiujitsu, more confident of myself. Soon, making mistakes in everyday life just wasn't a big deal. I was able to take down a dude that was six feet, three inches and 220 pounds, after all. Or if I made a dangerous mistake in class, I made amends with my instructor and classmate, talked through the problem, and didn't run out the door, never to return. I even went back the

---

next day and had the same partner. I took tests and earned belts as promotions.

When we moved away from that community, it was very sad and hard, but I had a goal to train and teach jiujitsu to my next community. That plan made the move hurt less. Then the pandemic happened, and we couldn't invite people to train. My husband went to a gym that said they were monitoring for illness, sanitizing, and safe, but my husband still brought home the virus. I have not trained for jiujitsu since.

In the process of writing this, I was able to see my sadness and grief around that. But I can also see very clearly, that if I hadn't been sick and unable to continue with my physical training, I might never have turned to writing about my suffering. I might never have started this book. But also, if I had never walked into that jiujitsu gym and gone through recovery from my perfectionism, I wouldn't have had the tools to listen to the small voice that told me to write. I might have ignored the voice that told me to do it anyway. In that gym, I developed the grit it would take for me to show up with brain tumor headaches and nausea and fatigue. This has been the hardest physical struggle of my life, and I needed the gifts that jiujitsu gave me to fully realize the gifts that this illness has given me. To realize these gifts is to glorify God.

The traditional definition for "glorify" is "to acknowledge and reveal the majesty and splendor by one's actions." When I was a kid and heard "Glorify God," I thought of a robed choir in a marble-y cathedral singing beautiful but formal hymns at the occasional event, such as Christmas or Easter. That's one way to do it. But it's also about finding the majesty and splendor in our everyday lives.

Because creativity takes on all forms—from the physical to the spiritual to the mental to the visual—we get to be a part of creation, of giving back to the beauty and power of living in this world. And we get to glorify God in all that we do.

We get to glorify God by being true to ourselves.

STEP TEN PRACTICE:
The God Jar

At some point in my recovery journey, someone suggested a God Box. After hearing about it for many years, I was ready to try it.

I didn't have a box. But I did have a jar.

Going through a bunch of my grandmother's old art supplies that she had left behind when she died was such a blessing. It woke up my creativity and gave me a priceless connection to her. She had saved these old calendar pages with pastel colors, pretty pictures, and quotes. I saved a few and then threw out the rest, but then, something stirred in me a few minutes later, so I snatched them back out of the trash. I tucked the pages away with no idea what I was going to do with them. The God Jar suggestion came not two weeks later. The papers were the perfect size for me to scribble notes to my HP, fold them up, and drop in my jar.

I scribbled my fear, my hope, my dreams, my worry, my secrets, my love—everything that comes up in my writing that I want to turn over to my HP but I don't quite know *how*. As the days passed, as my jar filled with beautiful, colorful little prayers, my heart filled with joy.

Here's my morning ritual:

1. I write my morning pages (aka, morning dump).
2. I say my morning prayer.

3. I sit quiet for a moment, pull out a few scraps of paper, and scribble my notes to my HP.

4. I fold up the papers.

5. If my candle is still lit, I pass the papers over the flame (but am careful not to light them on fire), and then I open my jar. I thank my HP for taking these fears and hopes and dreams from me, and I drop them in.

6. I go about my day.

After handing it all over to my HP, I am free to move on, knowing the Universe can work out the problems while I get out of the way. This will work even if you don't believe in God or an HP. It's a simple way to release anxiety and worry. You can name your God Jar "G.O.D." as in "Good Orderly Direction," or you can call it anything you want, even the "Here, you deal with this" jar will work. You can turn over your worry or plans or ideas to your deeper intuition and your higher self or subconscious to process while you go about your day.

It's a physical action of surrender to help you let things go.

CHAPTER ELEVEN

Making Meaning
Out of the Mundane

When I was little, I wanted to be an artist, that is until I found out that my Aunt Susie was a psychologist. And I wanted to be just like my Aunt Susie. In my eight-year-old mind (and in my forty-four-year-old mind, too), she had it all together. She was kind and gentle and asked me different questions than all the other grown-ups. I knew that I wanted to help people, to work with people. I had the opportunity to be a candy striper (hospital volunteer) when I was a teenager, and that's when I changed my mind—I wanted to be a nurse when I grew up.

But an abusive relationship and an already alcoholic drinking pattern aren't conducive to college, so I dropped out. The Navy seemed like a really good idea to get me the hell away from all my problems. My uncle and great-grandfather had served, so could I. You've heard the phrase "No matter where you go, there you are." Turns out I still had problems with men and alcohol in the Navy, which actually makes me giggle in hindsight given the fact that I could always "drink like a sailor."

The recruiter convinced me that instead of the medical field, I should go into the nuclear field because my test scores were so good. He said I could apply for nursing school "in no time" and nuke school would be a stepping-stone. "In no time" meant six years of stepping-stones, but I did get accepted into a program where the Navy sent me to nursing school. Going back to college in my late twenties was really fun in theory, and for a bit I was able to party like a college kid AND get all my work done.

But the longer school went on, the more I felt like maybe I hadn't made the best decision. I was really good at patient care, and I loved talking with families at the bedside, but the pressure of school and papers and single parenting and bills and untreated mental illness and binge drinking and debt was more than I could handle.

I still wanted to help people, and for a minute I thought I should be a drug and alcohol counselor (a lot of us do that in recovery). My first job out of the Navy, while I finished my psychology degree, was as a residential counselor at a locked-ward children's psychiatric facility. My patients were boys ages eleven to fourteen who had been labeled by the state as sex offenders, although for many of them, they were also victims of childhood sex abuse. This is not the best job for a newly sober, very shaky human being who is not quite sure how to do life just yet.

I have fond memories of working with those kids, but the trauma and the pain those children had faced and caused in their short lives were way too much for a newly sober person just trying to keep their own shit together. Still wanting to help but not sure how, I bounced around quite a bit. I worked in property management for a while. Then I worked with veterans and an awesome boss on a Marine Corps base. But then we moved to our next duty station.

My work was at home for a bit. Newborn twins and a toddler are a full-time job for two, and my other half was at work after two weeks of paternity leave. The kids grew up and I learned how to be an organized, mostly with it, stay-at-home mom. I made elderberry syrup and put laundry away after I folded it. I signed papers and packed lunches and got everyone to school. I worked in the house and on myself until they got home and then supper and bed and repeat.

Was this my purpose?

One summer, I was attending a writing retreat and we were talking about our dreams and purpose. Someone asked me, "So what do you want to be when you grow up?" I blurted out, "Preacher!" Without hesitating. I tried to take it back and stumbled over why I shouldn't be, when my friend looked me in the face and said, "I was waiting for you to realize that, Rev." My cheeks hurt from how big I was smiling and how right that felt, but also, how scary.

I found a seminary, applied, and was accepted, and then . . .

I got a job offer as a sixth-grade math teacher. My initial plan was to teach and go to seminary at the same time, while also writing this book, and parenting, and homemaking, etc. Something had to give. Seminary will happen after this season of teaching, but I find that I get to minister to kids all day long—and if there's any group that needs help, it's sixth graders!

FINDING OUR PASSION

Many of us hit bottoms in life because we lose sight of, or haven't found, our purpose and passion. We work nonstop to pay our bills and try to make a difference. It is truly a privilege to be able to stop and question our purpose, to seek out our passion. But let's stop and do that here, right now, together.

What is meaningful work? If you remember, during the pandemic there was a big thing about essential workers. There are undoubtedly jobs and roles that must be done so that we can go on living. Seeing the world screech to a halt in a matter of days showed us just how much we took certain jobs for granted. The drive-through workers and grocery store cashiers that many generally don't even notice became the glue that held our worlds together, not to mention the healthcare workers, teachers, and first responders.

I've spent so much time asking myself, What is my purpose? Over and over, I asked the Universe what I'm supposed to do, stuck on this idea that it had to be presentable, in a neat little package.

"What do you do?"

"Oh, I'm a [fill in the blank] and I [fill in the blank]."

And we hope that people see that we add value to the world because we "fill in the blank."

But the more I asked the Universe, the more I got the answers of "Choose joy" and "What are you passionate about?"

And then it hit me: I love it when I see a child working through something difficult in class and then the light comes on. I love it when I share my story with another woman in recovery and she has an aha moment or a revelation about her own story. I love speaking to a crowd and seeing heads nod and hearing the laughter of identification. The lightbulb moment. That's what brings me joy. That's what fuels my passion. But I also love the experience of my own personal lightbulb moments—learning a new craft, going faster or farther after hard work, pushing through resistance to write, mastering the trap and roll.

These moments make me feel joyful and alive.

So instead of asking, What do I do? or What is my purpose? try asking, What lights me up? and What fuels my passion?

You may find lots of little ways to ignite the light and passion in your day. The act of glorifying God is an act of celebration, a way of igniting that light. This is not a guide to achieving work-life balance by any means. If I'm honest, I think work-life balance is a bit of a sham, but I know that when we are living the principle of glorifying God in ALL that we do, there isn't much need for gimmicky life hacks, or "fill in the blanks."

LIVING OUR PURPOSE

My husband, Nick, has been in the Marine Corps for over twenty years, and when this goes to print he'll be officially retired. Between my teacher pay and his retirement pay, we can survive and be well, but I have a hunch that after a few months off, he'll find a job. I think we're meant to work as long as that work is meaningful to us. You know that cliché, "Find a job that you love, and you'll never work a day in your life." Well, that's bullshit, however, I think there's something to be said for finding meaningful work that helps us feel our full worth and value. The fact that we exist means we have inherent worth and value, but there's something about doing that thing we're meant to be doing at the right season of our lives (whatever that looks like to you). It just, as they say, hits different.

Nick says all he wants is to be happy at this point. I pray that he finds just the thing to fulfill that happiness.

After searching outside myself for years for my purpose, I've found it. Only after going within over and over was I able to find true worth and value in my work life. Not all of us get to retire from our first career and handpick the next, nor do we all get our calling in conversations at writing retreats. Sometimes we just have to work to get our paycheck so that we can live. And that can also be an act of glorifying God.

> Risk isn't equitable. But what we can do is the inside work and be open to what glorifying God in all that we do looks like right now in our workplaces.

It could be as simple as trying to be present with every customer. Or it could look like being kind to yourself when you make mistakes. It could look like clocking out right when your shift ends and not giving one more minute of your time than necessary. Does it look like finally having that hard conversation with your boss about your pay?

One of the hardest career changes that I've made was staying at home with our children instead of going back to work. I got six weeks' maternity leave with my firstborn, and I missed his first birthday because of military training. I had a job that I loved when I was pregnant with my second child, and it seemed right that I go back to work when he arrived. But getting him up and ready every day to have him taken care of by people who weren't me or their father, especially when it wasn't absolutely financially necessary, didn't feel good to me. So, Nick and I decided that I'd stay home. Then came this whole other set of feelings. What came up was this nagging sense that since I didn't make an income, I was a burden. I put all this pressure on myself. If I sat down for any period of time or, God forbid, took a nap, I felt I had to make up for that rest with more work. I had this powerful urge to tell my husband all that I accomplished at home while he was at work. My thoughts were plagued with the notion that if I wasn't making money, I wasn't worthy. The idea that if I'm not productive then I'm of less value still haunts me at times.

During this disorientation, a quote from Mother Teresa helped me forge my path: "If you want to change the world, go home and love your family."

With three small children in my home, having a sense of purpose didn't make the job any easier. But the gifts that show me I'm on, or close to, the right path have been plentiful. One afternoon, I was having a particularly difficult time regulating my nervous system—the kids and I were/are learning to do this all at the same time as I'd never learned this lesson at their age. (Seriously, seventies and eighties kids, did you ever hear any grown-up say, "Breathe," or, "Regulate your nervous system"?) I was sitting on the kitchen floor rocking back and forth through a panic attack when Mason climbed into my lap and reminded me to breathe by holding my cheeks, looking into my face, and showing me how to inhale and exhale, just like I had taught him to do.

It turns out that the work that happens at home with my family is some of the most important and impactful work I've ever done.

> I am raising the future. And the future is raising me right back.

My purpose has changed over and over again throughout the years. The big and small ways that we glorify God will also change over and over, from the mundane to the magical.

BUILDING A BRIDGE TO CHANGE

The biggest gift of this phase of my life with my husband and our children is that we get to finally plant roots in our community. Our fifteen-plus years of military life together (with thirty-four years of combined service) was divided into two- to three-year chunks where we never felt quite part of the communities because we were in a constant state of transience. As soon as we found friends and got into a routine, it was time to pack up and move again. While we made the most of it, there was still a shell of protection—don't get too comfortable, we'll be moving again soon anyway.

Now, we live in a small town, where community is very accessible. I never imagined I'd move back to my hometown, where everyone knows everyone, but at this point in time, I can't imagine anywhere else I'd rather be. Being a teacher in a small town can be a trip. I can't go to town or Walmart without seeing a handful of the kids I teach and their parents, and that's after just one year of teaching.

To truly plant roots in our community is to be of service to our community. This looks different for everyone. I've joined the NAACP and I run every charity road race I can find. I've started a local writing circle and volunteer to help with art summer camps. Service to community may be your actual job (teaching math to sixth graders is service for sure) or it may be the thing you do for fun. There's nothing that makes me feel more connected than being of service. There is ownership with service. It shows humility, and I believe it is glorifying the best of what God is—our love for one another.

Our love for one another is the bridge to change. A bridge is a structure that helps us get over an obstacle, like a river or a ditch, or even a problem, or a gap in services. A bridge is a connection from where we are now to where we want to be, and to build that connection, we have to work on building individual relationships. We are all part of a family, right?

At the beginning of the school year, we have an open house where students can come and walk the halls to find their classes and meet their teachers. I'm in my second year of teaching, but this was my first year attending open house as a teacher. The absolute best part of my night was having the kids I taught last year come and excitedly give me hugs, telling me all about their summers. What I did not expect was the tears that came to me when a particular student came and gave me a hug. He and I had struggled together in class, but I did my best to show him every day that despite what happened outside or inside my classroom, he mattered. At open house he didn't say a word, he just walked up and hugged me, and then walked away. But the fact that he was there meant I had made a connection, one that I didn't think was possible on our hardest days last year. By modeling the 3 Things in my classroom, I had given him a bridge, and that bridge was now going to carry him to seventh grade.

Building bridges is about being willing to make connections where you normally might not. It's being curious about one another's stories. Mama and my sister are always making fun of Daddy and me for talking to everyone wherever we go. I got this trait from him; I'm curious about the people I come across in my life and I want to know more. You don't have to become an extrovert (I'm surprisingly introverted), but connecting with others in our day-to-day life builds bridges.

At my aunt and uncle's wedding, they danced to "Bridge over Troubled Water." Years later, when I was a teenager, I found the album and listened to it constantly. Mama likes to refer to all the bridges over troubled waters she and Daddy have gone over in their lifetime together. One time she misphrased it and said, "There's lots of bridges under the water," and it stuck. There will be bridges under the water and bridges that burn. But leading with love, seeking connection, and finding community is how we change our world for the better.

If you are in a position of power, in my opinion, you are obligated to build bridges. Now, we all define power differently, but by building a bridge with someone who has less than you—less money, less resources, less love, less freedom—you can help them access the things they don't have. Your bridge isn't just an act of kindness, it's an act of equity. There is risk involved, there is always risk, but we can't let fear stop us from making connections.

Each morning, during the school day, we have a moment of silence during announcements. No one is made to pray (even in southern Georgia, y'all) but I utilize that time to do so, silently to myself. The seventh-step prayer from the Big Book is a good starting point for me and for being of service. It reads: "My Creator, I am now willing that you should have all of me, good and bad. I pray that you now remove from me every single defect of character which stands in the way of my usefulness to you and my fellows. Grant me strength, as I go out from here to do your bidding."

If we can approach daily work with a heart of service, and with the intent to build bridges, we will understand what it means to glorify God in all that we do.

STEP ELEVEN PRACTICE:
Pause. Breathe. Happy. Repeat.

The magic of pausing is that it allows us a brief moment to connect with our intuition, whether it's our breath or our HP. It's a good idea to have an outward symbol that reminds you to check in. I used to have a key on my nightstand and in my car—and now I have a tattoo of a key—to help me remember that the key is the willingness to continually surrender. A prayer or a favorite mantra helps too. The more you practice, the more natural it will become. Soon, you will find joy in working through those moments of agitation and doubt. Have you ever wished for a pause button? With this practice, you can have one! (It's not called practice for nothin' though.) Do it now with me.

1. **Pause.** Don't read ahead yet; just stop right here for a moment to be present. Feel your body in space.
2. **Breathe.** Take in a large, four-count belly breath in and sigh it out. In 1 . . . 2 . . . 3 . . . 4 . . . sigh it out.
3. **Happy.** You feel that? That little moment of separation where you can access your center?
4. **Repeat** this three times before you continue. Use this the next time you feel overwhelmed or agitated.
5. **Pause. Breathe. Happy. Repeat.**

Before going on to the next chapter, open your journal and choose an external symbol to serve as your reminder to pause, and write down a mantra or prayer for you to recite during your pause, connecting you to your ritual.

CHAPTER TWELVE

Let There Be Rest, Y'all

I've been guilty of dismissing play as kid stuff in the past. I'm the serious one. I love planning and lists and schedules. If I'm not careful I get grumpy and controlling when my routine falters for whatever "life happens" reason. My anxiety and a diagnosed phobia related to germs (emetophobia for as long as I can remember) may be at the root of this seriousness, as well as my choice of careers. When living in a constant state of hypervigilance, there's no time for rest, and play can seem impossible.

For a long time, I had a fixed idea that I am not a playful person (sober).

Instead, I decided that my husband was the playful parent, and that I was the nurturer. He can just jump up and start a game instantly with our children. I have to get in the zone, get out of my sympathetic nervous system, and figure out *how* to play, usually after I try to talk them into something less messy, and by the time I've gotten myself hyped up, they've moved on without me.

Dr. Stuart Brown wrote a book called *Play: How It Shapes the Brain, Opens the Imagination, and Invigorates the Soul.* In this book, he defines play as the "state of mind that one has when absorbed in an activity that provides enjoyment and a suspension of sense of time . . . [play] is self-motivated so you want to do it again and again."

Play is self-motivated. I'd never thought of it this way.

While exploring his book, I decided blowing bubbles might be fun. My kids got over it after a few minutes, but I stood outside until the bubbles were gone. I was able to relax and enjoy and give my nervous system a break from checking all the boxes. It's easy for me to go outside and be with my children if I have bubbles on hand. They end up bouncing on the trampoline and I give them bubbles to jump around in. These backyard bubble moments helped me realize how important it was to do things "just for fun."

When I got sick and turned to art for healing, it seemed so simple, yet miraculous, how good art was for my soul. When I painted watercolors, I felt at peace, and afterward, I felt renewed in a way that I had not experienced before. I thought if watercolors were this amazing, maybe I would like to make T-shirts and vinyl crafts—turns out those things were fun too. But as I started collecting hobbies, something interesting happened. I shifted from using art as a way to play and made it into a way to be productive. I started figuring out ways to monetize it and make more stuff in less time. I made wreaths and ornaments and cute pouches and upcycled items found at thrift stores or discarded materials. My art sessions turned into work sessions, and they left me drained and confused. Why wasn't it fun anymore?

I couldn't wait for my first craft booth at our local annual Wild Chicken Festival to come and go so I could go back to making art for fun. That Wild Chicken Festival was the rainiest, windiest day of the season. The weather held back just long enough for me to set everything up and make one sale—a cute tray I'd found at a thrift store and painted. We had to pack up between downpours. I boxed it all up and felt completely defeated. I stuck everything in the attic because I didn't know what to do with it, all wet and disorganized. And folks, that's where it sits to this day.

Rest and play help us reconnect to our bodies and to our HPs. When we're out there doing and being productive, we are putting our energy into the world. We need time to go internal and plug into our source. We need time to tap into joy and fun, so we can fill up our hearts and our cups. Rest and play are how we learn what it means to glorify God in all that we do.

THE POWER OF PLAY

So, you may cringe at the idea of watercolors or making T-shirts with cute sayings, but maybe creating a multicolored spreadsheet to organize summer activities is your idea of a good time. Peter Gray at the National Institutes of Health says, "The characteristics of play all have to do with motivation and mental attitude, not with . . . the behavior itself. Two people might be throwing a ball . . . or typing words on a computer, and one might be playing while the other is not. To tell which one is playing . . . you have to infer from their expressions and the details of their actions."

> We can turn any activity into an opportunity for
> playing.

Take a minute to think of what you consider to be play. I love nothing more than going out for a long run with a bunch of other moms (clunky strollers and all). I also love a well-organized road race (the running kind, not the cars kind)—the crowd, the swag, the accomplishment, the high fives, all of it. My husband goes purely for the exercise. He will never run another marathon. He would rather throw around heavy stuff all day than run another mile.

Our tweenager loves to sing, dance, and act. Their play spans from belting out pop songs in their room, to performing short stand-up sets at the table during dinner, usually stuff they learned from TikTok, but still play, nonetheless.

It only counts if it is play for you. I realized the other night that *Wheel of Fortune* and *Jeopardy!* with my parents and husband are some of my favorite moments of the week. We get competitive and joke about cheesy game show banter and cheer each other on. I love podcasts that are a mix of comedy and true crime, but my mom is horrified by the idea. The point is that play is wholly personal, it just has to feel like play to you.

Do you think of sex as play or a chore (we've all been there, *amiright*?)? There's nothing more fun than when my husband and I sneak off to have what we call "grown-up time" or "nap time" while the kids are occupied and both of us are into it.

And speaking of naps, like real naps—not code for sex naps—my bed is one of my favorite places. I get all snuggled up on a Saturday or Sunday (maybe after a code word "nap time," if I'm honest) with a good book and lots of pillows. I could read until I fall asleep and that is fun to me! Nick would think he'd wasted a day, but that is my favorite way to play—with or without bubbles.

REST IS THE ULTIMATE GLORY

I had my craniotomy to remove a brain tumor at Emory University Hospital in Atlanta. Dr. Barrow and his team are amazing. We drove up Friday morning (surgery was on a Tuesday) for pre-op. While getting bloodwork, COVID testing, and an EKG, I asked the nurse, "Is the COVID test still up the nose?"

She turned to me serious as a heart attack and said, "Nope. Up the butt."

Deadpan. It landed so perfectly, we both cackled. I had tears I was so tickled. (It's still up the nose, by the way). And when I took off my mask for the swab, she gasped, "My God, you're gorgeous!"

Nurses are angels on earth. It could have been just a nervous sweaty painful pre-op, instead, I had a joyful connection with a beautiful human. Thank you, Nurse Jordan.

Waiting for surgery and prep, they played the Indigo Girls. I remember looking around trying to hear the music. Relieved, I finally did hear "Closer to Fine" right before the staff got my attention again and sent me off to sleep. The next thing I knew, I was awake in recovery and in pain, but also in shock that I was awake and aware that I had just had brain surgery. And I have to say that's how I felt for my entire hospital stay. All three days of it. Awake, aware, in some pain, and in shock (the good kind) that I had just had brain surgery. There were zero complications and the only reason for me to be in the hospital after day two was observation and pain management. I was good to go. I had surgery on a Tuesday and was discharged on Friday.

At home, I slept and slept and slept. I woke up to eat and say hi to my family, and then I slept some more. I felt like an infant. That was the first week home. The second week I was up more and in more pain. More swelling and icing and laughter and activity. Still couldn't believe I'd had brain surgery and was doing so well. I started walking to the mailbox and then the stop sign with my walker. Then, I ditched the walker. Then, I walked for fifteen minutes. Then twenty. I was doing really well.

And then the honeymoon ended. I think it was the first big rainstorm that did it. I couldn't smell the rain (loss of smell is a side effect of my surgery). Dolly's words—that we find glory in the rain smell—hit me hard.

My lack of motivation became bigger than my desire to heal. I began to wake up with horrible questions rolling around in my head: Will I ever stop sleeping eighteen hours a day? Will I ever want to paint or write again? Will I ever be able to smell the rain? Will I ever be able to enjoy food again?

I couldn't believe how much I'd taken for granted, how much my sense of smell added to my life. So, I sat in my grief. I complained, dragged my journal out, and did my best to start my writing practice again. Every time I tried though, I would fall asleep immediately after my morning pages. But I kept at it. My sister started telling me how everything smelled on our walks, and just in general. That act of kindness helped so much.

I kept walking. I kept going. And I did eventually stop sleeping eighteen hours a day. I still can't smell the rain per se, but I remember its glory, and though food has taken on a new sensation in my life, I still love it, and have begun to renegotiate taste without flavor.

Look, I don't want to Pollyanna this whole thing. It has been hard, and there are days when it is still hard. I am not magically better; I am slowly recovering. But I am doing it with all the support, glory, rest, and faith I can muster around me.

Have you seen the quote slides going around social media that say something like "The opposite of faith is fear"? You may have heard it in church or in a twelve-step meeting. When we show up, feel the fear, do the thing, don't die, and then we keep going, THAT is faith. That is celebration. Continuing on with our work, play, and rest even when it's scary and hard, THAT is faith. Celebration of life happens when we use the gifts we've been given and when we remember all the gifts we still have.

The tumor is gone. And I still have all the stuff in me that I learned from the process, but especially the importance of rest.

THE POWER OF DOING NOTHING

My grandmama's name was Rosalee—that's my mama's mama. She, like Grandmother, oozed creativity, just in a different way. Grandmama would make lists for everything, solving all the world's problems from her recliner. She was a writer; she contributed to a column called "Of Shoes and Ships" in our town's weekly paper for years and years. She threw elaborate parties with handcrafted favors. I absolutely loved hearing her tell stories and visiting her antique store, pretending I was in another time. Before my time, Mama says she was a Rosie the Riveter but with munitions during the war. But do you know what my Grandmama was best at?

Resting.

She would stay in her housecoat, reclining in her chair, sometimes listening to old Southern Gospel tapes or CDs. Sometimes she would tell herself, "Come on Rosie, time to get up," and those around her would smile knowing that she would not in fact be getting up anytime soon. She was so good at resting that we've dubbed those days as "Rosie Days."

On top of that, Rosie had a group of friends who had been together for years. They would meet up and throw parties and meet for fellowship. And they called themselves the "Do-Nothing Club" because a lot of times they met to do, well, nothing.

Oh, to have Do-Nothing Clubs where we get together and play and rest? I think Rosie Days and Do-Nothing Clubs should be adopted by everyone because we could all use a good recliner.

I am a nap person. I have always been a nap person. For many years I tried to ignore that I was a nap person because those around me were not nap persons and it's hard to stop everything and go lay down when those around you don't need naps or they don't honor sleep and rest as a necessary part of life. I think some of us are wired for more sleep than others. My husband stays up late and wakes up early. He rarely needs a nap. I can go to bed early, wake up late, and still need a mid-day rest. For many years, I shamed myself for wanting rest. Thank God my sponsor Michele is also a nap person and gave me permission early in my recovery to rest.

After years of finding all of my fun and play in running races and working out, my brain tumor journey showed me how to find real rest. Since I lost much of my former physical abilities, my face and body are different than before. Weight has been stored, which I believe is a form of protection and survival. Regardless, I've learned how to accept these changes and the knowledge that my body knows what it needs.

> Running a marathon isn't going to help me heal
> right now, but being kind and gentle with myself is.

On the seventh day, he rested . . . Most major religions have a sabbath day or a holy day reserved for worship, rest, and reflection. This isn't a novel self-care trend; the ancient religious texts stress the importance of rest. We must have time to clear our channels and to rest our over-cluttered minds. It's good for us, for everyone. Rest is our divine right. And when we rest, we allow others to feel like it's okay to rest. Rest for the sake of resting, rather than to get back out there and produce. Being of better service is a result, sure, but just as it is with play, doing nothing for no other reason but to rest is glorious.

As the deadline for my final draft of this manuscript loomed, my dad was rushed to the hospital and nearly died. He was diagnosed with sepsis and kidney failure and atrial fibrillation. We had to go three hours away to Atlanta (back to Emory) because all the hospitals in the major cities and towns of southern Georgia had no available beds. After two weeks of hospital time with surgery on his knee (the source of the sepsis) and several other procedures to keep him on the healing route, he came home to our house. He's been bedridden or in a wheelchair during this process, but he's doing his best to get up and walk with the walker to build his strength and stamina back.

This morning, I was helping Daddy do his walking. He made it all the way to the living room, probably forty feet total! After I got him settled back into bed, I asked him about his pain and how he felt. "I'm okay," he said with a shrug. I dug deeper and asked how he was feeling spiritually. He confessed, "I'm tired of being an anchor, of holding everyone back." I asked him to think of how he would respond if one of his priest friends or parishioners had said the same thing to him.

"Well, I'd tell them that it was their turn to rest, to heal and accept help from people who loved them." Ah yes, there you have it. It is your turn to rest and heal and accept help, especially from a power greater than our own.

We also talked about how the 3 Things, how being part of a family, being true to ourselves, and glorifying God in all that we do, are part of a cycle. They feed into each other, with one allowing for the next to grow in strength and love and light.

When I was heavy into distance running, and illness or fatigue set in on a day that I should have been working out, resting felt like quitting. The idea of being a quitter cued old core memories that I couldn't finish anything, that I was a pee-pee pants failure, that I wasn't good enough. Now, I look at it as quitting—a little bit. Today I quit and rest. The deadlines and training plans of tomorrow will take care of themselves only if I take care of myself. It's easy to forget to play and to minimize the need for rest when we're out there doing and being productive.

> When you need to, drop your pack, the load of
> day-to-day life. Take your rest. Then pick up your
> pack and keep marching along when you're ready
> to keep going.

Rest and play are important for their own sake—not only so we're more productive when we do get back into action. Our nervous system unwinds, and we get back to our bodies and connect to our source/GUS/Jesus/God. Rosie Days and "do-nothing" days are important so that we can connect with our true selves, our HP, and we can know peace and serenity.

Listen to good ol' Southern Gospel, or the Indigo Girls, or the sound of the rain (something I love to do, even though I can't smell it right now)—just take the time to go internal and plug into your source. Tap into and reclaim your joy and passion. Rest and play are how we learn what it means to "Glorify God in all that you do."

STEP TWELVE PRACTICE:
The 3 Things Exercise

When I was preparing for brain surgery, I had a very hard time with the thought of my family worrying to the point of suffering during the wait. I was at peace and comforted by the 3 Things. In fact, I wrote the entire first draft of the manuscript in the days leading up to surgery. When I wasn't writing, I spent some time praying to ease the suffering for those who were spending so much time caring for me and helping me through my own physical pain. What came was the idea for a mini 3 Things retreat. It was a surprise, tucked away in envelopes waiting for them after I went to Emory. My husband brought me their creations to admire when I was in the neurosurgery ICU recovering from surgery. Now, I've taken what I created for my family and am sharing it with you too.

1. You are part of a family. I offer you the following prayer to remember the people around you, both your family of origin and the wonderful circles of community dancing around you.

A Prayer for You

Please be with us all this day. Guide our hands and our feet, that we may tap into intuition and embody the 3 Things in our lives. May we remember that we are part of a family, give us the courage to be true to ourselves, and help us celebrate life today with rest and play. Help us each do our part in healing so that we may know collective recovery. Thank you for my family and friends that are my family. For all the sentient beings. In all these things we pray.

If you'd like, write your own prayer about your family and community.

2. Be true to yourself.

Make a list of twenty things that you want to do. Don't stop until you have AT LEAST TWENTY. Here are some questions to get you going:

If I knew anything was possible, what would I try?
If I had all the money in the world, what would I do?
If I didn't care about looking foolish, I would . . .
In another life, I would have . . .
I used to do ___ all the time and miss it.
I've always wanted to . . .
People my age don't . . .

Now, write twenty things.

When you are done with your list, review it and see what you might be able to start when you get back home. Pick at least one thing and promise to yourself that you'll give it a try.

3. Glorify God in all that I do. Now we're going to play. Either paint or make a collage or both that depicts the you that you felt when you were imagining those twenty things. Pick one and paint that thing or pick a feeling and make that. Collage a vision board to remind you of your list.

We did it! We are now on the path to collective recovery together. I'm honored that you've made it this far. Please take a moment to admire and reflect on your experience. How can you make the 3 Things your own? Do you have a better understanding of community, contemplation, and celebrating creativity in your own life?

Go back through your art journal and take in what you've completed. If you decided to read cover to cover before delving into the exercises, consider going back to try the exercises from the beginning. Please share your work on social media with the hashtag #The3Things. It'll be just like when I saw my family's art in the ICU, but even better because it'll be shared with our biggest family. <3

Conclusion

When I was a kid, I felt special because I heard my family saying I would one day be next in line to be a priest. I think deep down I believed them and secretly wanted to do that but didn't believe I was worthy as I lived out my teen years. At this point, I can't say for sure whether or not it will happen, but in a way, I've been preaching my whole life. I mean, after I saw Nadia Bolz Weber, I was like, wait if she can be a Lutheran pastor, then I could be an Episcopal priest. (If you don't know who that is, put down your book for just a sec and google her). But then there's the whole Jesus miracles thing and some of the actual Christians that I have a really hard time with, so I'm not there yet, okay HP? Regardless, my relationship with my HP is changing day by day. I've explored and applied to and been accepted to an interfaith chaplaincy seminary. I will pursue that when writing and teaching math aren't center stage anymore. Mostly, I'll be spending my time doing the next right thing for my community, my true self, and my creativity.

If this experience has taught me anything, it's that life is short, and I don't want to waste it doing anything that isn't true to myself or my values. I don't want to spend time othering myself or finding ways that I don't belong. And I don't want you to do that either.

The path to collective recovery is an individual trail that gets us all free together. Sometimes I find myself off the path. I feel lost, full of doubt, and unmotivated to do any of the practices that got me this far.

Sometimes you have to get off the path to see where the path lies. We aren't going to do this perfectly. Healing is not linear, and neither is living the 3 Things.

When we embody the 3 Things, we will lead with love. We will help one another through this life even as it feels like the world is telling us we have to do it alone. We will envision and bring about a world where we can all stand in our true selves, where my truth doesn't keep you from living in your truth. We will live in such a way that there is enough for everyone, and we will generously acknowledge each other's humanity with grace. We will allow each other, and especially ourselves, to be messy humans, free from perfectionism and judgment. We will learn to celebrate our creativity and the light that it brings us. We will enjoy the winding path of healing and recovery, and we will embrace play and rest along the way. We will have Rosie Days, and Do-Nothing Clubs, and we will quit just a little bit until we can pick up our packs and continue on our paths. We will come to know collective recovery. We will be part of a family, we will be true to ourselves, and we will glorify God in all that we do.

Thank you for joining me on this path. I'm so glad that you are here.

ACKNOWLEDGMENTS

This book would not be possible without my husband, Nick. Thank you for all of the hours of playing interference with the kids so I could write, and for all of the times you gently nudged me to actually write when I was stalling. You've always been a champion for whatever and wherever my whimsies take me (us) and for that I am so grateful. Thank you, my love.

To the boy who made me a mama, my sweet baby James, I'm so proud of the man that you have become. Thank you for the short story you wrote for me on Mother's Day—it came at a time when I was doubting my ability to complete this project, and you showing up on the page inspired me to keep going. Thank you for loving me—I love you so!

To Mama and Daddy, thank you for being my biggest fans and for all of the talks around the supper table when I got stuck in the story. "All because two people fell in love" takes on more and more meaning as we age, doesn't it?

To Clayton, Mason, and Marshall, the joy you bring to my life is worth all of the gray hair. Thank you, children, for being so wonderful.

Thank you to my sister, my first and forever best friend, Kelsey, for dropping everything to help, every time I needed you. (We've got to stop having reasons to drop everything though, okay?)

To my brother, John, for knowing what I need to hear and when. I'm still jealous that you got to go to St Andrew's, but hey, I got to write this book because of it—so thanks for graduating, brother.

To Michele L., thank you for teaching me how to vote for myself and for sharing your tree of self-acceptance. I love you to pieces.

Jessica F., for all of the calls I missed because I was distracted with the book (or the kids), I apologize. Thank you for your patience and for being the best hype person a girl could ask for.

To all of the sober women who have held me up over the years, you helped me write my story.

Amy Miranda, thank you for reminding me of what we've forgotten.

To all of my Rise Writer family: Nada, Emily, Hilary, Ryan, Amy, Liana, Jayne, Alyson, Jill, Melissa, Jenna, Jackie, and Tammy—and all those I've left unnamed—thank you for writing the good fight with me.

To Rebekah Borucki, thank you for your 11:11 periscopes, your coaching sessions where you told me to feel the fear and do it anyway, and for sending me Kristen.

Jamie Lou, you are the kindest editor a girl could ask for.

Jen Pastiloff, I will be forever grateful for your gift of people connecting.

And last but not least—Kristen McGuinness, you are *the* reason this book survived the past three years. Thank you for believing in *The 3 Things*. Thank you for your kindness, generosity, and wisdom from 20,000 years in publishing. Thank you for all of the coaching, and the calls, and I mean *all* the calls, and the laughter, especially the laughter that kept us from crying, and of course the crying too.

BIBLIOGRAPHY

Alcoholics Anonymous Big Book. 4th ed. (New York: Alcoholics Anonymous World Services, Inc., 2002).

Brown, Brené, *The Gifts of Imperfection* (Minneapolis: Hazelden Information & Educational Services, 2010).

Brown, Brené, *Braving the Wilderness* (London: Vermilion, 2017).

Brown, Stuart L and Christopher C. Vaughan, *Play: How It Shapes the Brain, Opens the Imagination, and Invigorates the Soul* (New York: Avery, 2009).

Cameron, Julia, *The Artist's Way: A Spiritual Path to Higher Creativity* (New York: TarcherPerigee, 2016).

DeMent, Iris. "Let the Mystery Be." Recorded 1992. Track 1 on *Infamous Angel*. Rounder, CD.

"Getting Back to Civil Discourse Will Require Americans to Be Vulnerable and Humble." n.d. AAMC. https://www.aamc.org/news/getting-back-civil-discourse-will-require-americans-be-vulnerable-and-humble.

hooks, bell, *killing rage: Ending Racism* (New York: Henry Holt and Co., 1996).

Portnoy, Gary. "Where Everybody Knows Your Name/Theme from Cheers" Recorded by Charles Burrows 1982. On *Cheers: Music from the TV Series* [CD]. Paramount Network Television.

ABOUT THE AUTHOR

MAGGIE BOXEY—Navy veteran and teacher, she serves children at the middle school in her hometown of Fitzgerald, Georgia, where she lives with three of her five children, her Marine husband, and their three cats and pitbull mix named Jack. Her passion for equity in her community has led her to serve on the board of directors for SOWEGA Rising, a Black-led nonprofit for progress in Southwest Georgia. She's been sober and in recovery for seventeen years. When she's not preaching, teaching, or being of service, you'll find her running in the country, painting watercolors, cuddling with Jack, or vying for the cats' (who prefer her husband) affection.